12374

CHEMAWA

INDIAN TRAINING SCHOOL

Indian Training School,
Salem. Ore.

1879 – 2000

Away from Home:

American Indian
Boarding School
Experiences

EDITED BY MARGARET L. ARCHULETA,
BRENDA J. CHILD, AND K. TSIANINA LOMAWAIMA

PUBLISHED BY THE HEARD MUSEUM   PHOENIX, ARIZONA

© 2000 by the Heard Museum.
Second paperbound printing with revisions, 2004
Third paperbound printing, 2009
All rights reserved.
ISBN 0-934351-72-4

Distributed by Museum of New Mexico Press, Santa Fe

Printed in Canada by Friesens Printing

Interviews conducted by Tessie Naranjo and Margaret L. Archuleta
Designed by Carol Haralson
Copyedited by Erin Murphy
Coordinated by Lisa MacCollum, Creative Director, Heard Museum
Photography credits and photograph sources are listed on page 144.

This book is a gathering of many voices. The editors would like to thank all of the authors for their part in the whole.

John Bloom's essay on sports in Indian boarding schools is adapted from "'Show What an Indian Can Do': Sports, Memory, and Ethnic Identity at Federal Indian Boarding Schools," and W. Roger Buffalohead and Paulette Fairbanks Molin's essay on American Indian families at Hampton Institute is adapted from "'A Nucleus of Civilization': American Indian Families at Hampton Institute in the Late Nineteenth Century," both published in 1996 in the *Journal of American Indian Education,* volume 35, number 3.

Additionally, the Heard Museum would like to thank the writers and publishers who gave permission to reprint the following in this publication:

"Gia's Song," by Nora Naranjo-Morse, from *Reinventing the Enemy's Language: Contemporary Native Women's Writings of North America,* edited by Joy Harjo and Gloria Bird, published in 1997 by W.W. Norton & Company, Inc., New York.

Excerpts from *Ora Pro Nobis (Pray for Us),* by Oskiniko Larry Loyie, from *Two Plays about Residential School,* published in 1998 by Living Traditions Writers Group, Vancouver, British Columbia.

"Indian Boarding School: The Runaways," from *Jacklight,* by Louise Erdrich, published in 1984 by Henry Holt and Company, Inc., New York.

LIBRARY OF CONGRESS CATALOGING-IN-PUBLICATION DATA

Away from home : American Indian boarding school experiences / edited by Margaret L. Archuleta, Brenda J. Child, and K. Tsianina Lomawaima.

      p. cm.

  Includes bibliographical references and index.

  ISBN 0-934351-72-4

  1. Off-reservation boarding schools—United States—History. 2. Indian students—Relocation—United States—History. 3. Indian students—Government policy—United States. 4. Indians, Treatment of—United States—History. 5. Discrimination in education—United States—History. 6. United States—Race relations. 7. United States—Social policy. I. Archuleta, Margaret, 1950- II. Child, Brenda J., 1959- III. Lomawaima, K. Tsianina, 1955-
E97.5.A93 2004
371.829'97—dc22

                2004047416

PHOTOGRAPHS

Cover: Untitled, n.d., oil on canvas, 27⅛ x 18⅛ inches, by Angel de Cora, Winnebago (1871–1919).

Half-title page and back cover: Train arriving at the Chemawa Indian School, Salem, Oregon, ca. 1900.

Title page: The arched entrance to the Indian Training School (Chemawa) at Salem, Oregon, 1886.

This publication was made possible by the generous support of The Rockefeller Foundation. A special thank you goes to Tómas Ybarro-Frausto at the Foundation for his continued support of the project and his understanding of its importance. This publication was produced in conjunction with an exhibition, *Remembering Our Indian School Days: The Boarding School Experience,* which was funded by the National Endowment for the Humanities. The exhibition opened November 18, 2000, at the Heard Museum.

BEGINNING IN 1879, TENS OF
THOUSANDS OF NATIVE AMERICANS
LEFT OR WERE TAKEN FROM THEIR
TRIBAL HOMES TO ATTEND INDIAN
BOARDING SCHOOLS, OFTEN LONG
DISTANCES AWAY. SOME
STRUGGLED BITTERLY. SOME
SUFFERED IN SILENCE. SOME
SUCCUMBED TO TUBERCULOSIS OR
INFLUENZA AND LOST THEIR LIVES.
OTHERS FLOURISHED AND BUILT A
NEW SENSE OF SELF WITHIN A
WIDER WORLD, WHILE PRESERVING
INDIANNESS IN THEIR HEARTS.

THIS BOOK IS DEDICATED
TO THEM ALL.

CONTENTS

surely there were as many experiences as there were students—are important pieces to add to the giant patchwork quilt that is known as America's history.

The first off-reservation Indian boarding school was founded in an old army barracks in Carlisle, Pennsylvania, in 1879. Indian boarding schools were but one part, albeit an extremely important part, of the United States government's comprehensive policy of attempting to assimilate its Native peoples into mainstream culture. The idea behind this assimilation policy was to "kill the Indian to save the man," that by placing "the savage-born infant into the surroundings of civilization" the Indian would "grow to possess a civilized language and habit" (Prucha 1990). This misguided policy has had a devastating and lasting impact on Native peoples throughout America. Theirs are human stories filled with tears, tragedy, and lasting pain, as well as laughter, perseverance, and joy.

The exhibition *Remembering Our Indian School Days: The Boarding School Experience* is a "first-person" exhibition: The experiences of boarding schools are shared with us by those who were students there. They ask us not to forget what they experienced. They remind us that, in the end, the goal of cultural genocide failed. Ultimately, the story of Indian boarding schools is one of personal survival and cultural triumph.

Frank H. Goodyear, Jr.
Director, Heard Museum

AWAY FROM HOME

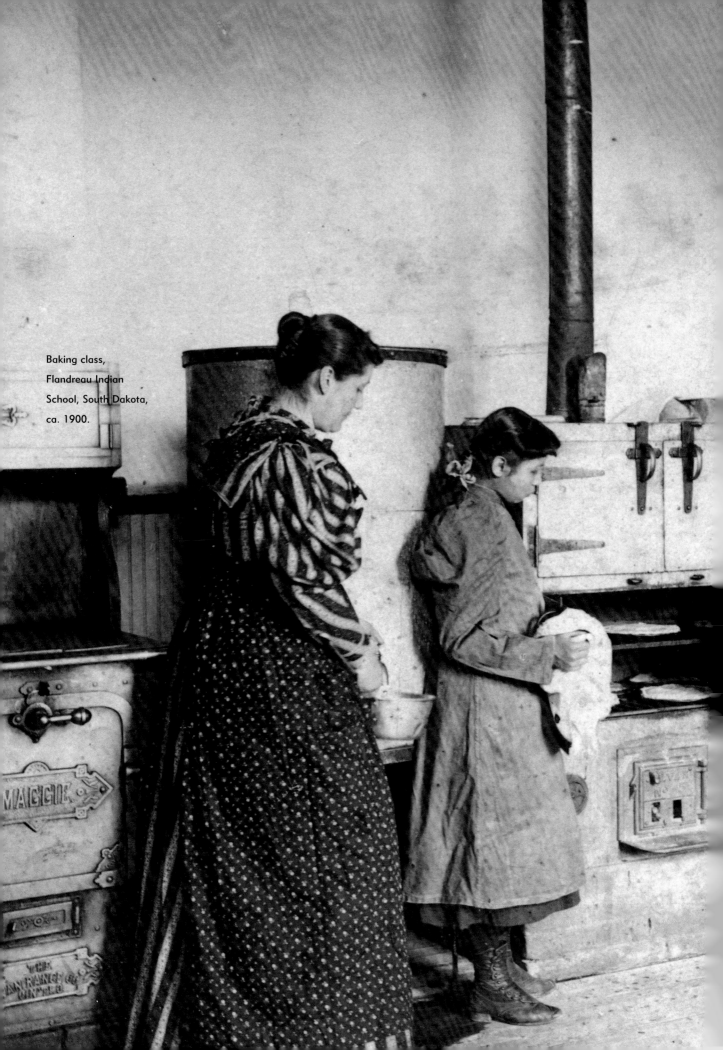

Baking class,
Flandreau Indian
School, South Dakota,
ca. 1900.

INTRODUCTION

MARGARET L. ARCHULETA,
BRENDA J. CHILD, AND
K. TSIANINA LOMAWAIMA

The boys took what little there was and what little they had and made it into something bigger and finer and stronger than they had found.

BASIL JOHNSTON, OJIBWE, 1989

IN 1879, LUTHER STANDING BEAR, LAKOTA, arrived at Carlisle Indian School uncertain and courageous. He was among a group of children who had been "recruited" from the recently hostile Lakota tribes as essential hostages, taken far from home to Carlisle, Pennsylvania, to guarantee their parents' and communities' "good behavior" and cooperation with federal agents. His enrollment was an act of personal bravery and sacrifice (Standing Bear 1975). At the turn of the last century, Polingaysi Qöyawayma, Hopi, who soon received the name "Elizabeth White" in school, defied her mother and snuck away to the Third Mesa day school, fascinated by the cotton dresses

[15]

Pine Ridge Indian
Boarding School,
South Dakota,
ca. 1891. Many
families set up
camps near the
schools in order
to have contact
with their
children.

Indian girls, Phoenix
Indian School,
Arizona, early
1900s.

Christine Begay,
Navajo, Miss
Sherman 1999.

distributed to the girls, and intensely curious about this new and alien institution (Qöyawayma 1964). In 1999, "Miss Sherman" Christine Begay, Navajo, told an interviewer her reasons for attending Sherman Indian School: "I live in a white society and it wasn't working out for me right. It wasn't about my personality or who I was inside, it was the outside of me they judged. I felt comfortable with all these other Indians here so I stayed here[.] I came back every year" (Heard Museum 1999).

As Luther's, Polingaysi's, and Christine's stories reveal, students' reasons for attending the schools have been as diverse as the students themselves. Many Native children were removed from their homes by federal officials, while families tried desperately to evade or oppose mandatory school enrollment policies. Other children were eager to enroll—motivated by curiosity, the desire to learn, comforted by the familiarity of schools that their grandparents, parents, aunts, uncles, and siblings had attended. Some families sent children away reluctantly, because of parental death or disability, poverty, the hardships of reservation life. Others would have gladly chosen local education in day schools had they been available, but they were not, and many public schools would not enroll Indian children prior to World War II, so boarding schools were the only educational "choice" available. A Cherokee woman who entered Chilocco in 1939 said that Indian parents "sent their kids there because they wanted them to get an education." She continued, "It helped many, many people, thousands of them. There weren't school buses then, or money to board kids in town . . . so many just wouldn't have gotten an education at all. . . . It really was a marvelous school; I've always felt indebted for my education there" (Lomawaima 1994).

The history of Indian boarding schools in the U.S. began in the seventeenth century, when mission schools, boarding schools' precursors, first opened. The mission schools were subsidized by the U.S. government from 1810 to 1917. The government established a federal school system for Native Americans in the 1860s and in 1879 opened the first off-reservation Indian boarding school, Carlisle Indian School in Carlisle, Pennsylvania.

Carlisle's founder, army officer Richard Henry Pratt, summed up the key to "civilizing" the Indian: "Kill the Indian and save the man" (Prucha 1990). Pratt had experienced success with a group of Indian students in Hampton, Virginia, when he had enrolled them at Hampton Normal and Agricultural Institute, a school for African Americans run by former missionary Samuel Chapman Armstrong. (Today the institution is Hampton University.) Encouraged by his experiences with the

Before and after: Zie-wie Davis, Crow Creek Agency Lakota, 1878 and 1879. Zie-wie, age 15, was one of the first nine Indian girls at Hampton Normal and Agricultural Institute.

Hampton group, Pratt lobbied the federal government to support a federal school at Carlisle, with the goals of assimilating and acculturating Indian children by removing them from their families and communities and submersing them in the white man's world.

Carlisle was just the beginning. Within a few years, the government began building large, off-reservation boarding schools across the western United States. In 1884, the government built Chilocco Indian Agricultural School in Indian Territory (which became Oklahoma), Genoa in Nebraska, and Haskell Institute in Lawrence, Kansas. Chilocco was for many years the flagship

She is shown upon her arrival (left) and four months later (right). Before and after photos of students became important documentation that assimilation and acculturation were working at the schools. Zie-wie's expressions betray the staged setting.

school for agricultural instruction, while Haskell's commercial business courses trained generations who worked for the Bureau of Indian Affairs in Washington, D.C., and field offices across the country. Carlisle, Haskell, and Chilocco had diverse, multi-tribal student populations, but other federal schools enrolled only locally or regionally. Santa Fe Indian School in New Mexico, established in 1890, primarily enrolled students from Southwestern tribes and pueblos. Sherman Institute in Riverside, California, enrolled California Indians, as well as many Hopis from Arizona. Chemawa Indian School, established in

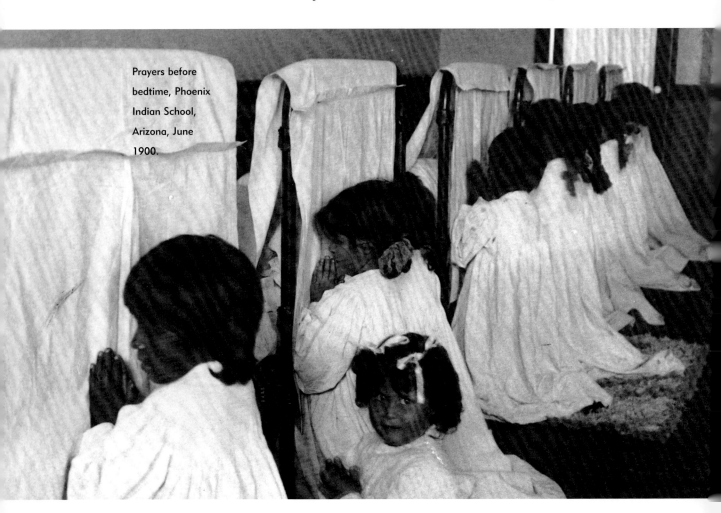

Prayers before bedtime, Phoenix Indian School, Arizona, June 1900.

1880 as the Indian Training School, now located near Salem, Oregon, enrolled students from the Native Northwest. Phoenix Indian School, built in Phoenix, Arizona, in 1891, drew its students from the twenty-plus tribes in Arizona. Over the years, student enrollments waxed and waned. Schools had to recruit from more remote areas to maintain enrollment levels after World War II, as public education became more accessible to Indian people.

In the 1950s and 1960s, for example, Chilocco enrolled many Navajo students from the Southwest into the special Navajo Program, and also heavily recruited Alaskan Native students. Many boarding schools were closed in the 1980s, but a few remain: Haskell is now Haskell Indian Nations University, and Chemawa, Sherman, Flandreau (South Dakota), and Riverside (Anadarko, Oklahoma) still operate as high schools.

Indian boarding schools were key components in the process of cultural genocide against Native cultures, and were designed to physically, ideologically, and emotionally remove Indian children from their families, homes, and tribal affiliations. From the moment students arrived at school, they could not "be Indian" in any way—culturally, artistically, spiritually, or linguistically. Repressive policies continued to varying degrees until the 1960s, when activism, reassertions of tribal sovereignty, and federal policies supporting tribal self-determination began to impact educational institutions and programs. Today, the majority of Indian children attend public schools, but the federal school system is still in operation and includes day schools, on-reservation boarding schools, off-reservation boarding schools, and Haskell Indian Nations University. In Canada, mission residential schools remained the core of the educational system for First Nations people until the schools were closed in the 1980s.

Arriving at school, Riverside, California, ca. 1940. The method of transportation evolved from horses and wagons to trains, buses, and automobiles, but students' feelings of isolation, despair, fear, and separation upon arriving at the schools did not change.

Federal programs to eradicate "Indianness" sometimes, in some places, and for some people, have been successful—and that is a tragedy. Despite this, and despite other tragic effects of assimilative policies and institutions, Indian people, families, communities, and cultures have survived. That is a miracle. Former student Ruthie Blalock Jones, Delaware/Shawnee/Peoria, said of the schools, "They were started to stamp out the Indian from the Indian, you know, make us all into white people, and you know, it didn't work. Actually . . . it was the exact opposite: It made us stronger as Indian people. It made us more aware of and more proud of who we were" (Heard Museum 1999).

In the following pages you will find stories of the strategies of human survival—resistance, accommodation, faith in oneself and one's heritage, the ability to learn from hard times, to create something beautiful and meaningful from scraps and fragments. You will find stories of familial love, student friendships, and even devotion to schools. As Pablita Velarde, Santa Clara Pueblo, said, "I appreciate the Indian school for even being there, even if it wasn't the greatest of schools at that time. At least it was there"

Train arriving at
Chemewa
Indian School,
Salem, Oregon,
ca. 1900.

(Heard Museum 1999). These stories tell us about individual experiences and more as well, for the institutional life of boarding school is a common thread running through American Indian history.

From the 1870s through the present day, Indian children from thousands of homes, from hundreds of diverse tribes and reservations, have entered federal or mission boarding schools. They came because they wanted to; because their families wanted them to; because some judge or social worker or probation officer or federal agent decreed they had to. They came as young as four or five years old; they came as young adults. They came practicing Native religions or they came as Baptists, Catholics, or Episcopalians. They came speaking Muscogee, Lakota, Hopi, Ojibwe, Choctaw, Navajo, or any one of the several hundred indigenous languages of this country. Some came speaking only English. The only thing they all certainly had in common was going to Indian school. ⌒

GIA'S SONG

BY NORA NARANJO-MORSE

Thung joo Kwa yaa na povi sah
Thung joo Kwa yaa na povi sah
    T'say ohi taa geh wo gi wa naa povi sah
    pin povi
    pin povi do mu u da kun
    ka nee na nun dun naa da si tah.
On top of Black Mesa there are flowers
On top of Black Mesa there are flowers
    dew on yellow flowers
    mountain flowers I see
    so far away that it makes me cry.

Phoenix Indian School, Arizona, ca. 1900.

She opened her eyes slowly,
    to awaken from a trance
        caught by a song,
           transporting her to childhood,
Back to the flowers
    growing atop Black Mesa,
    so far and yet clearly brilliant.
Awake from the song,
    Gia focused on her daughter,
    anxiously awaiting
    to be taught a new song.
The old woman chose to take her time,
    she had learned from experience,
    attention is better paid by children,
    when there is a little pause,
        and mystery
           in storytelling.

Soon enough Gia spoke . . .
    "When I was a young girl,
    my family would camp
    below Kwheng sa po,
    during the farming months.
    We spent most of our days
    following my grandmother
    through rows of corn
    and playing in the streams below.
    One day white men came in a wagon,
    telling us about a school for Indians,
    run by the government.
    We were told this school would educate
    and prepare us for jobs in the white man's world.
    None of us knew what any of it meant, but these men spoke
    sweetly
    offering grandmother a ball of baling wire
    for each child that went to school.
    Before we knew what was happening,
    we were sitting in the back of their wagon,
    on our way to government school,
    away from our families,
    to another man's world.
    Often we would cry,
    out of loneliness,
    but this song helped us
    to remember our home."
Gia thoughtfully straightened
the pleats on her skirt,
swallowing the last of her coffee.
Smiling, she continued . . .
    "The government school taught sewing,
    I learned on an electric machine,
    By the time I returned to the village I could
    sew, but few of the people had heard of sewing machines,
    or even electricity.
    The machine I learned to operate as my trade
    could not be carried here and there,
    but this song you are learning,
    will always be carried in your heart,
    here and there."

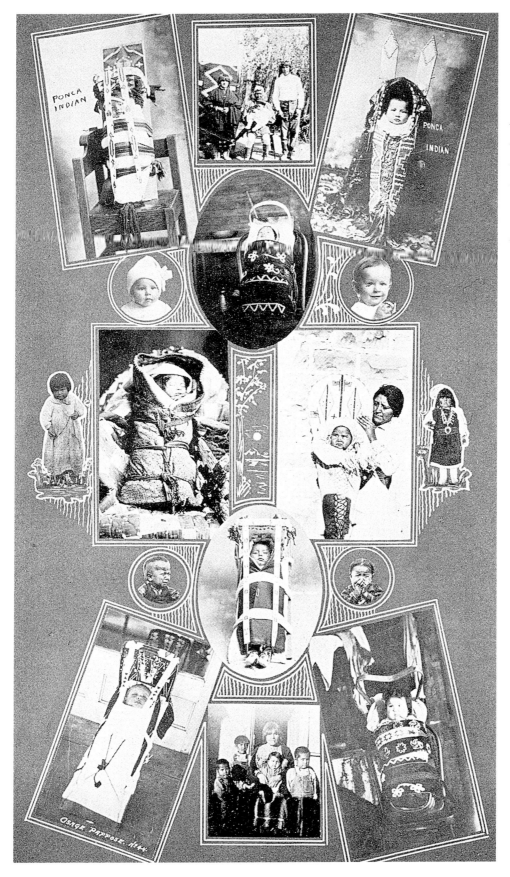

Photo collage of Indian children, 1916, published in *The Red Man, An Illustrated Magazine Printed By Indians*, a monthly publication of the Carlisle Indian School Press.

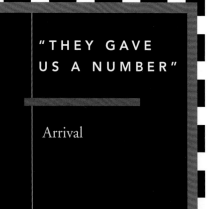

"THEY GAVE US A NUMBER"

Arrival

It was **very difficult** for me at first, for students at the school were not allowed to speak **the language of the Indians.** At the time I understood nothing else.

WAYQUAHGESHIG (JOHN ROGERS),

WHITE EARTH OJIBWE (ROGERS 1974)

Indian Training School (Chemewa), Salem, Oregon, 1886.

THE ENTRANCE TO NEARLY EVERY INDIAN BOARDING school is marked by an arch, a symbol of the transition from "uncivilized" space to "civilized" space. As new students arrived at school and passed through the arch, they essentially passed from one life to another, entering a difficult and traumatizing time that, for many, marked numerous difficult and traumatizing years. Former students vividly recall their first hours and days after passing under the arch, when they were often assaulted by practices consciously designed to strip them of their identities. This is how the schools began their task of creating a new kind of individual.

Entrance to
Indian Training
School (Chemawa),
Salem, Oregon,
1885.

1583 – ENTRANCE TO INDIAN TRAINING SCHOOL, CHEMAWA, NEAR SALEM, OREGON.

At the beginning of every school year they inoculate you, and they lined us up just like you do in the Army, I used to say, like cattle, and I remember I had five inoculations. . . .

And I was so homesick, and sick, I just thought I would die. That's one of the earliest things I remember. And another early memory was of being finecombed for lice. . . .

They had a little metal comb and it had short teeth, real fine teeth.

CHOCTAW WOMAN, STUDENT AT CHILOCCO INDIAN SCHOOL, 1930S (LOMAWAIMA 1994)

Chilocco Indian Agricultural
School, Oklahoma, 1938.
Students designed the
"swastika"-style logo atop the
arch in the 1920s, drawing on
Southern Plains artistic motifs.

We got off the bus in this strange, strange place, and they didn't even tell us we was going to have to stay, and we thought we were going to stay just for the night, you know, so we went in, and I laugh now but at that time it was so scary . . . walking together, you know, whimpering, and we got into this government girls building, and the first thing I could remember was smelling the floor varnish.

PATRICIA WACONDA, KICKAPOO/LAGUNA (HEARD MUSEUM 1999)

Little girl's school uniform, Sherman Indian School, Riverside, California, ca. 1927. Uniforms for both girls and boys were a part of daily life at boarding schools, beginning at Carlisle Indian School under Pratt, when boys at Carlisle dressed in wool military uniforms and girls wore heavy, Victorian-style dresses. Students sewed the uniforms as part of their domestic and vocational training.

From the moment they arrived, students were immersed in the regimentation, discipline, uniformity, and highly scheduled life of the school. Strict military discipline was the rule, although reforms led to a relaxation of some military aspects beginning in the 1930s. Students were stripped of their "home clothes," issued government regulation clothing and uniforms, fine-combed for lice with kerosene, bathed, and had their hair cut. They were prohibited from speaking Native languages, wearing Native dress, or participating in any practice of cultural traditions—including singing, praying, dancing, and creating art—and were subject to severe punishment for breaking the rules. Students who came to school with Native language names were given appropriately "civilized" English names such as those of noted American citizens such as Ulysses S. Grant or George Washington.

Arrival at boarding school meant that brothers were separated from sisters, as boys and girls were kept strictly apart. In the 1930s, boys and girls were finally allowed to sit at the same tables together in the dining hall, an innovation that provoked anxiety as well as delight. Younger and older sisters or brothers were also often separated, as the dorms were age-graded. Students devised elaborate codes of slang and became expert note-passers to circumvent school rules that impeded communication.

When they first took us in school, they gave us government lace-up shoes, and they gave us maybe a couple pair of black stockings, and long underwear, about a couple of them, and . . . slips and dress. Then they gave us a number. My number was always twenty-three.

LILLY QUOETONE NAHWOOKSY (NÜMA-NU 1981)

Drill corps, Phoenix Indian School, Arizona, ca. 1915.

Military trophy, Phoenix Indian School, 1929.

Before 1935, in the military days of the boarding schools, students were separated not only by gender and age for housing and classes, but also were organized into companies by gender and size for marching in close-order drill every morning. Sunday drill competitions resulted in treats for the winning companies. Students marched to parade music for visiting dignitaries, at public events in neighboring towns, and at world fairs. A Cherokee man who was enrolled at Chilocco in 1926 described the military-style drills:

"[The little boys were] in the Ironhead Platoon. They line 'em up by size, regardless of age, and they had these little guys, we called 'em Ironheads. Some of 'em were so young, they were five or six years old, and their patience isn't that great, so that's why we called 'em Ironheads. . . . We started drilling at five o'clock in the morning, one hour before breakfast. . . . I later joined the Marine Corps, and did twenty-eight years with the Marine Corps, and you hear people talk about how tough boot camp was, that was a breeze after Chilocco!" (Lomawaima 1994)
—LOMAWAIMA

Little girls' playground, Crow Agency, Montana, n.d. There were some surprising exceptions to boarding school repression of Native cultures. In several schools on the Northern Plains, little girls were allowed to recreate camp life during playtime. One of the tipis on the left appears to be covered with a gingham tablecloth.

Homesickness was intense for many, and the first few weeks of school were usually marked by extraordinarily high rates of students running away, "going AWOL," in the parlance of the schools. As revealed in the following pages, students faced an uphill struggle adapting to boarding school life. Regimentation, homogenization, and boredom pervaded the schools. Academic "standards" were quite low, and much of the day was consumed by work details. ⌒

Our name isn't supposed to be Jones [but] Chonku, [or] something like that and the teachers couldn't say it right so they just give us Jones.

WALTER B. JONES, BORN 1926, SANTEE SIOUX, ATTENDED FLANDREAU (HEARD MUSEUM 1999)

Kindergarten class at
Riverside Indian
School, near Anadarko,
OK, 1901.

"When you first started attending school, **they looked at you**, guessed how old
you were, set your birthday, and gave you an age. Then they'd assign you a
Christian name. Mine turned out to be Fred."

Fred Kabotie, Hopi, born 1900. attended Santa Fe Indian School 1915-1920
(Kabotie 1977)

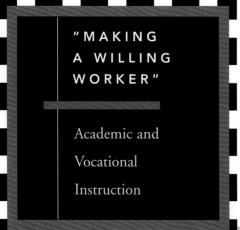

"MAKING
A WILLING
WORKER"

Academic and
Vocational
Instruction

Vocational training of the type offered at Indian Boarding Schools should prepare Indian youth for **effective citizenship** more efficiently than any other method known. Indian youth is **naturally shy** and timid and needs to come in contact with tradesmen, tools, materials, and processes . . . in order to make the adjustments necessary for **social efficiency.**

CHILOCCO INDIAN AGRICULTURAL SCHOOL, 1934 ANNUAL REPORT

DAVIDSON, PHOTO.
No. 42.

Indian Training School, Forest Grove, Oregon,   CARPENTERS AT WORK.   Capt. M. C. Wilkinson, U. S. A., in Charge.

Carpenters at work, Indian Training School, Forest Grove, Oregon, 1880. In carpentry classes at the boarding schools boys learned how to build houses, barns, and classrooms.

Several of the schools were built by students, and most were maintained by student labor.

FEDERAL INDIAN SCHOOLS WERE MODELED after the pattern of Christian missions, established as early as the 1500s in Mexico. Missionaries and government workers believed that Indian people, especially Indian men, were naturally inclined to idleness. Even Indian women, stereotypically perceived as "drudges," the hewers of wood and haulers of water, needed to be retrained in the appropriate domestic arts of a "civilized" household. Accordingly, schools incorporated training in the skills and values that policymakers felt were the foundation for independent citizenship, and thus did not focus as narrowly on academic subjects as other schools did.

Inasmuch as the purpose of the school is to train Indian youth for citizenship, THE STUDENT WHOSE RECORD IS NOT SATISFACTORY AS TO PERSONAL CONDUCT WILL NOT BE RECOMMENDED FOR GRADUATION.

CHILOCCO, OKLAHOMA: SCHOOL OF OPPORTUNITY FOR INDIAN YOUTH

Until the 1930s, boarding schools were organized on a half-day schedule that put students in the classroom for only a few hours a day, and so-called "academic instruction" was largely remedial and restricted to the lower grades. Even when off-reservation boarding schools such as Phoenix, Chilocco, and Haskell became high schools (in the 1930s and beyond), their curriculum stressed vocational and domestic instruction.

At the end of the nineteenth century, the Indian Service attempted to standardize its schools' curricula. Estelle Reel, superintendent of Indian schools, crafted the *Uniform Course of Study for the Indian Schools of the United States,* which was distributed in August 1901 to all Indian schools (as well as to U.S. colonial jurisdictions in Puerto Rico and the Philippines). Reel's goal was to train the Indian child to meet "the demands of active life, making him a willing worker as well as an inquiring learner" (Reel 1901). The *Uniform Course* was probably used by some teachers and ignored by others, and by the 1910s Reel's successors once again lamented the lack of a standardized curriculum.

ESTELLE REEL

An ardent suffragist and astute politician, Estelle Reel (1862–1959), shown here ca. 1900, was the first woman nominated to a political position high enough to require Senate ratification. In 1898, President McKinley appointed her superintendent of Indian schools, responsible for the hundreds of federal boarding and day schools, on- and off-reservation, a position she held until 1910. Reel believed in the racist ideology of her time: Indians (and other colored races) were inescapably conditioned by heredity and environment to be less than whites. She told a newspaper reporter in 1900:

Allowing for exceptional cases, the Indian child is of lower physical organization than the white child of corresponding age. His forearms are smaller and his fingers and hands less flexible; the very structure of his bones and muscles will not permit so wide a variety of manual movements as are customary among Caucasian children, and his very instincts and modes of thought are adjusted to this imperfect manual development. In like manner his face seems stolid because it is without free expression, and at the same time his mind remains measurably stolid because of the very absence of mechanism, for its own expression (Lomawaima 1996).

Reel believed that Native people were destined to labor in the fields, farms, shops, and homes of white America, and she often praised the "dignity of labor." She professionalized the Indian Service teaching corps, introduced summer in-service teacher training institutes, and crafted the *Uniform Course of Study for the Indian Schools of the United States.* —LOMAWAIMA

Blue Monday, Crow Agency Boarding School, ca. 1890. Both boys and girls worked in the school laundries.

UNIFORM COURSE OF STUDY

Superintendent of Indian Schools Estelle Reel believed that Indians were "too dull" ever to excel intellectually. In her *Uniform Course of Study for the Indian Schools of the United States,* distributed in 1901, she focused on trades training for boys, such as shoe making, and devoted a large part of the course to a domestic curriculum for girls.

Reel's instructions to teachers were intensely practical and incredibly detailed, as seen in this description of how sewing should be taught: "In the first year: Never permit sewing without a thimble. Do not let children make knots in thread. See to it that all sit in an erect position, never resting any part of the arm on the desk. Biting threads must never be tolerated.

Drill in use of thimble, length of the thread, threading needle, motion of arm in taking stitches, fastening thread; drill in the use of emery and holding scissors" (Reel 1901).

Other parts of the *Uniform Course* recommend exercises for "marching, breathing, calisthenics, and games" so that children would get the "requisite muscular exercise." Clearly, curriculum was not concerned with academic or intellectual development among Indian children. The goal was to produce subservient, docile, and physically regimented Indians who would follow federal directions.

—LOMAWAIMA

I got pretty adept at making pillowcases, but we really did things that were used there. I think I spent half a semester hemming dishtowels, and I graduated to pillowcases. I don't think I ever got beyond pillowcases!

CHOCTAW WOMAN, ENTERED CHILOCCO IN 1933 (LOMAWAIMA 1994)

In reality, over most of the years since the 1870s, teachers in Indian schools have struggled with poor materials or no materials at all, devised their own courses, and patched together curricula. These efforts have been united across generations by four commonalities: their intent to eradicate Native languages (despite some sporadic attempts in the 1930s to introduce bilingual materials, particularly in the Southwest); their concentration on the basics of the "Three Rs" (reading, writing, and 'rithmetic); their assumption that Indians would not aspire to or be fitted for higher education or professional training; and their emphasis on "practical" education.

Bobbin lace-making pillow, Hampton Museum, Hampton, Virginia, ca. 1900. Bobbin lace-making is a complicated process in which silk thread is wrapped and tied into delicate loops and knots that form the lace. Silver pins are used to hold the threads in place. This type of lace-making was taught at the schools at the turn of the century. *The Hampton Leader*, September 22, 1916, referred to a class of over a hundred students on the Oneida reservation, taught by a Mrs. Webster, that produced lace and cut-work "of the highest quality, equal to the Italian."

Sewing class, Flandreau Indian School, South Dakota, ca. 1900.

One of the things that made America great was **perseverance**, and that you learned there [at Indian school]. That's a lost art in society today. . . . They instilled that feeling of **pride**. Work was honorable, and you get out and hustle for what you get. . . . It was a great experience. You have a feeling of brotherhood that you just don't have going to public schools. —CHEROKEE MAN, ENTERED CHILOCCO 1929 (LOMAWAIMA 1994)

Oh [you worked off demerits] on your hands and knees, with our old wool sweaters. They made excellent polishing cloths [laughs]. You could see yourself in the floors of Chilocco . . . and as you walked you thought, "Oh, I wish I could fly!" and you dusted your tracks out as you went along. —CHEROKEE WOMAN, CHILOCCO STUDENT IN 1929 (LOMAWAIMA 1994)

The schools' vocational training reflected federal intentions to fit Indian people into the lower economic sectors of American society as small-scale farmers, manual and unskilled laborers, or domestic workers. Boys learned trades such as shoe and harness making, painting, masonry, carpentry, plumbing, commercial-scale baking, and agriculture (raising beef and dairy stock, and producing poultry, grain, and hay). Girls were enrolled in domestic science courses including child rearing, sewing, foods and cooking, and home nursing.

Learn to Earn at Haskell, ca. 1956. Vocational training was emphasized at the schools throughout the first half of the twentieth century. By the 1950s industrial vocations had replaced agrarian trades. Boys were likely to be trained as welders and girls as secretaries.

Student-made table, Hampton Museum, Hampton, Virginia, ca. 1895. This is an example of the beautiful and functional craftsmanship developed at early schools.

Despite federal intentions to provide credible training, most schools were limited by economic needs and rooted in economic pragmatism. Congress never appropriated enough funds to fully support the schools, and so student labor and the sale of the products of student labor were critical to keep the schools going from year to year. In 1928, when the secretary of the interior commissioned a study of the work of the Indian Service, per capita rates to fund schools were painfully low. Federal Indian schools received $225 per student per year; the only state school for Indians (in New York) received $600; and the very cheapest private school for non-Indians received $700 (Meriam et al 1928). Students baked pies, built and repaired buildings and furniture, washed and ironed laundry, fixed uniforms and shoes, ran power plants, milked cows, grew and harvested crops, ran printing presses, cleaned acres of buildings, and polished miles of corridors. Some students learned skills that were useful to them all their lives, but much of the labor was unskilled, repetitive drudgery.

Trades training for boys and domestic training for girls lagged behind the job skills necessary for many employment opportunities. Schools taught harness making as American industry and agriculture became mechanized. Only a small percentage of boarding school graduates ever made a living at the trade they learned in school, but many did go on to meaningful employment, and many alumni report satisfaction at having learned the American "work ethic."

Ironically, one of the main employers of boarding school graduates in the twentieth century was the boarding school system itself. Although the number of jobs was limited each year, boarding schools were ideal training grounds to produce workers for boarding schools. By the 1950s and 1960s, federal school officials were more concerned with providing accredited high school academic training, but an emphasis on vocational education—auto repair, electrical engineering, commercial business, or pre-nursing—remained intact.

One unique aspect of Indian schools' vocational training was the "outing program," first developed by Carlisle founder Richard Henry Pratt. "Outing" meant that teenage boys and girls were placed in rural homesteads and middle-class urban households to work as farm hands and domestic servants. Outing, more than any program, segregated the work of Indian children and pronounced them best adapted for the lower rungs of the American economic hierarchy. It reinforced lessons that the students were already receiving about the value of menial labor, in the classroom and through long hours of work in and around the school; girls instructed in household economy, for example, were told to picture caring for "a family on a limited

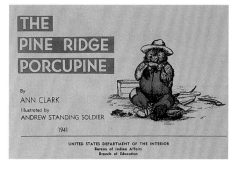

When policies shifted to a greater acceptance of cultural-based learning, the Bureau of Indian Affairs Board of Education developed a series of bilingual readers. Several were illustrated by well-known Indian artists of the time.

Ruth Edwards and brother, Hopi, holding Nancy, summer 1930, Phoenix, Arizona. Students in the outing program worked during school holidays rather than returning home. They did not visit their families for long periods, often as long as four years.

OUTING CONTRACT

Haskell Indian School's contract for outings, ca. 1900 (Child 1998):

1. Pupils absent under outing must observe all the rules of the school and be honest, industrious, and helpful to their employers.

2. Must bathe at least once a week and be neat and clean in personal appearance.

3. Must take care that their conduct and speech are always proper; must write home at least once a month. Should attend church as frequently as is consistent with their duties.

4. Must not be absent without the knowledge of patron, and in case of girls, without being accompanied by patron or some responsible person.

5. Must take proper care of their clothing and must spend judiciously any money (not to exceed one-half of their earning) paid to them direct by their employer; must be saving.

6. Must be kind, courteous, helpful, and agreeable to those about them, in order to obtain the greatest benefit of their outing; boys must not gamble or use tobacco or liquor.

7. Must not leave their employer without his knowledge and approval of the school. In case of trouble the pupil should write the school and await instructions. (Child 1998)

income." Carlisle's assistant superintendent enumerated the benefits of outing this way in 1900:

> It gives a command of the English language, a knowledge of family life, of business methods, of farming, machinery, and stock, and above all the consciousness of ability to make a living in any civilized community; of not being a dependent, but a valued member of society, and a factor in the labor market. (Child 1998)

Through the outing program, boarding school officials encouraged students to enter the homes of a white American middle class and, like a sponge, soak up their values. Simultaneously, they were expected to dedicate hours of labor to surrogate families while strategically being separated from their own relatives and kin. Boarding schools actively sought an alternative to sending students home to their communities during holidays and summer vacations, fearing the consequences of long retreats with parents and relatives. The outing program solved this pressing dilemma.

Superindent Reel's *Uniform Course* praised the program, saying it placed the student "in the midst of the stir of civilized life, where he must compete with wide-awake boys and girls of the white race," and continuing, "Association with good white people is the best civilizing agency that can be devised" (Reel 1901). Carlisle's declarations of success encouraged other schools, and female students at Haskell worked as maids in Kansas City under the aegis of outing as late as the 1930s. More than one Haskell girl felt exploited by a job "too hard," or with "too much responsibility" for meager wages. Cynthia Duffna, sent from Haskell to the Kansas City home of a shoe store manager and his wife, outraged her employer simply by sitting in the living room after company arrived and setting a place for herself at the dinner table. Her employer scathingly reproached, "Cynthia does not know her place." She left her job after little more than a week (Child 1998).

The experience of outing student Bernice Dupris illuminates the reasons administrators wanted to prevent students from returning home during holidays. Dupris went to work for a Kansas City family who lived close to a streetcar line, where she lived and cared for two toddlers. Although the good-hearted mother treated Bernice kindly, making her "feel at home," Bernice "wept ever since" her arrival. The two children stirred memories of home, and whenever Bernice looked upon their young faces she was reminded of her own "small brothers and sisters" (Child 1998).

Boarding school students who participated in outing had mixed feelings about the program, though many teenagers appreciated the small pocket money it offered. In the early days of government boarding schools the outing program was praised in Washington for advocating "family values," even then a bit of political rhetoric and subterfuge that privileged the majority, this time at the expense of Native American families.

We LEARN to WORK and EARN MONEY

Victor, Sherman Indian School, Riverside, California, ca. 1950. The goals of assimilation were present in every aspect of students' lives. Everyone, from the youngest to the oldest, had a job.

We Learn To Work and Earn Money, Sherman Indian School, Riverside, California, ca. 1950s. This photo collage illustrates the varied skills that boys and girls learned as part of their outing experience.

The gravestones shown read:

EARNEST

DORA
DAUGHTER OF
GRAVY BULL
SIOUX
APRIL 2? 1888

NORA
RANCHO
NOVEMBER 15 1886

HELEN
YOTSAYA
APACHE
APRIL 29 1890

AARON
YATOSEK
APACHE
AUGUST 30 1888

GODFREY
BLATCHA
APACHE
JULY 31 1890

FANNY
CHARGINGSHIELD
SIOUX
MARCH 7 1892

NANNIE
LITTLE ROBE
CHEYENNE
FEBRUARY 15 1895

WADE
AYRES

HENERY OURA

ALBERT
HENDERSON
FOR
SEPTEMBER 15 1880

COOKING
LOOK
ALASKAN
JANUARY 4 1904

ROSE
POPS
APRIL 30 1891

DORA
MORNING
CHEYENNE
JUNE 2 1891

ELI
HUNLONA
APACHE
MARCH ? 1895

SUSIA
NACH KE.
APACHE
MAY 14 1889

Children's graves, Carlisle Indian School, Pennsylvania, 1991. The school cemeteries are solemn reminders of the children who did not survive the boarding schools. At the turn of the century, influenza and tuberculosis epidemics hit the schools hard, killing hundreds of children.

IN THE EYES OF AMERICAN INDIAN FAMILIES, children away at boarding school faced two serious risks to their health. One danger was disease, especially trachoma, influenza, and, most menacing of all, tuberculosis. The second was homesickness, which deeply affected the mind and spirit. Either peril was alarming.

Parents worried when children grew inconsolably lonesome for home, and the concern was magnified when serious diseases threatened young and precious lives. Especially when a student was ill, a web of relationships grew among student, parent, and the school superintendent who was responsible for informing families of student illness. A series of letters from 1929 about an Ojibwe boy named Charlie reveals something about these relationships. Charlie, a student at Flandreau, came down with rheumatic fever, and the school superintendent wrote to Charlie's parents on Minnesota's Leech Lake Reservation.

Phoenix Indian School Hospital, Arizona, ca. 1896.

Sac and Fox Tuberculosis Sanatorium, Toledo, Iowa, late 1800s.

TUBERCULOSIS SANATORIUMS

The late nineteenth and early twentieth century history of boarding schools is closely interwoven with that of tuberculosis sanatoriums. Hundreds of students fell victim to deadly tuberculosis within the close confines of boarding school, and most American Indian TB victims languished in segregated sanatoriums. Sick students at Flandreau and Haskell, for example, moved to Sac and Fox Sanatorium in Toledo, Iowa, or Sioux Sanatorium in Rapid City, South Dakota. The latter, known as "Sioux San," was a deplorable institution that Indians viewed as the equivalent of death.

Government officials and physicians did not comprehend the contagious nature of TB early on, and so they failed to separate sick children from the rest of the student body. It was thought that the students came down with TB more often than the rest of the American population because of Indians' physical inferiority; they were widely believed to have poor constitutions and to lack natural vitality. As Estelle Reel wrote, "There can be little doubt that many of the children enter school with inherited tendencies to disease, particularly to tuberculosis, and special efforts have been made to prevent its development in pupils thus predisposed" (Reel 1907).

Scientists and physicians eventually gained more understanding of the contagion, and this information slowly filtered down to the Indian schools. Indian parents appear to have understood the connection earlier. They wrote to boarding school officials, encouraging them to watch for signs of illness in the children. —CHILD

Sherman cemetery, Pierre, California, ca. 1950. This cemetery was closed when the boarding school began to send seriously ill children home. Although present-day Sherman is located in Riverside, the original Indian school was in Pierre, an adjacent community.

> This is to inform you that your son Charles is quite sick. He has a high fever and the doctor says he has rheumatic fever. He is not in danger now but I thought it might be well to tell you so you would get it first hand and not through some of the students who sometimes write in such a way that it alarms parents. We have a good nurse and a good doctor and he is well cared for. We do not feel that it will result in anything more than this and if he should become more serious, I will advise you at once. I will let you know later when he is getting better.—Flandreau superintendent, 1929 (Child 1998)

News arrived painfully slowly when parents knew a child was sick. Four days after the superintendent's letter was drafted, Charlie's mother, concerned about her son, wrote back to him. Her letter exposed the tangles and lags of communication common in rural America at the time, but also clearly manifested a powerful determination to watch the progress of his illness and stay informed. Distance did not imply that mothers and fathers ceased being parents.

> I thank you very much for writing me about Charles being sick. I was so terribly worried about him that I went up to Cass Lake and wired you asking how he was, but got no answer, did you get the telegram? The agent may be didn't send it. Then I had Mr. Allen phone to you this morning and found that my son was some better. In case he should get worse wire Mr. Allen and he will phone me from there as we cant get no message here by wire.—Ojibwc woman, 1929 (Child 1998)

Charlie stayed at boarding school after his illness, and his mother continued to worry, scrutinize, and monitor his health from northern Minnesota. She became alarmed a year after the rheumatic fever scare, when her son seemed unhappy, tainted by the spiritual malaise common among boarding school students.

My son, Charlie, seem to be discontented at the school, & what am I going to do about it? He has written to some friends here that he don't like it there. And if he feels that way, don't you suppose its best for him to come home? As I think he won't do any good to stay there. I would like you to talk to him, he is very tender hearted, and if you will speak kind to him & advise him to stay there & be a good boy, not think about running away from the school, tell him that I figured on him learning some trade while there, so to make a living for me, when he left the school. And I feel very much disappointed in him not liking the school. I am afraid that some boys are coaching him to run away, as he always has been a good Boy here at home, I don't think he would do anything like that without someone putting himself to it. Do what you can with him for me.—Ojibwe woman, 1929 (Child 1998)

Although Charlie, like most students, recovered his good health, cemeteries at Carlisle, Chemawa, and Haskell document that sorrowful outcomes were sometimes part of the boarding school story.

Singing class, Carlisle Indian School, Pennsylvania, ca. 1890.

Guard House at Indian School, Carlisle, Pa.
(built by the Hessians 1777).

Pub. by U. S. Lease, Carlisle, P

Well, we had a boys' advisor. . . . He was an Eskimo from Alaska and he ruled that dorm with an iron hand. Everybody was afraid of him.

BEN ZUREGA, CHIRICAHUA APACHE STUDENT (HEARD MUSEUM 1999)

Guardhouse at Carlisle Indian School, Pennsylvania, 1910. Hand-tinted souvenir postcard. The Guardhouse at Carlisle was often used as a site for corporal punishment. It was a bleak place with long, narrow, vertical windows that provided little light.

Boarding schools could be violent places, and abuse and neglect also devastated students' physical and emotional health. Violence, abuse, and neglect stemmed from the boarding schools' entrenched commitment to erasing Indian identity. Not only were children removed from their parents, often forcibly, but they had their mouths washed out with lye soap when they spoke their Native languages; they could be locked up in the guardhouse with only bread and water for other rule violations; and they faced corporal punishment and other rigid discipline on a daily basis. In addition to these intentional practices, schools also fostered more insidious violence: gang warfare between tribes, the "belt lines" boys had to run, and the sadism of dormitory advisors or "disciplinarians."

Less frequently told are the stories of sexual abuse. These stories are whispered today but seldom mentioned publicly. In the book *Reinventing the Enemy's Language*, Bernice Levchuck illustrated the ways these betrayals affected every moment of students' lives:

Intimidation and fear were very much present in our daily lives. For instance, we would cower from the abusive disciplinary practices of some superiors, such as the one who yanked my cousin's ear hard enough to tear it. After a nine-year-old girl was raped in her dormitory bed during the night, we girls would be so scared that we would jump into each other's bed as soon as the lights went out. The sustained terror in our hearts further tested our endurance, as it was better to suffer with a full bladder and be safe than to walk through the dark, seemingly endless hallway to the bathroom. When we were older, we girls anguished each time we entered the classroom of a certain male teacher who stalked and molested girls. (Levchuck 1997)

It always seemed like everytime I wanted to talk about this sexual abuse, it seemed like nobody wanted to listen. . . . It hurts, it really hurts! It's a tough thing to have to live with. **I want to put it out in the open,** to talk about it, 'cause I want to deal with it, I need to deal with it. . . . I was really scared to come out into the world, because of the way I felt, a lot of shame.

EHATTESAHT (NUU-CHAH-NULTH TRIBAL COUNCIL 1996)

First Nations people of Canada, like Ehattesaht, have in recent years begun to confront the issues of physical, mental, emotional, and spiritual abuse in the residential schools.

Private tales of terror became part of a national dialogue as a result of court cases filed in British Columbia, and in the 1990s the government of Canada issued a public apology for the residential school system, which was abandoned in the 1980s. In the United States, these issues have remained more private, as individuals, families, and communities struggle with the darker legacies of boarding school life.

Going Home, 1992, by Judith Lowry, Mountain Maidu/Hamowi-Pit River. In December 1916, eleven-year-old Molly Lowry, the artist's great-aunt, ran away from the Greenville Indian School, California, with four other homesick girls. Even though Molly's home was not far from the school, she died from exposure in the snowy woods between Greenville and Susanville (Dobkins 1997).

"WE SHARED A BROTHERHOOD"

Connections to
Family and Home

ONE VERSION OF BOARDING SCHOOL HISTORY is expressed in the story of Sun Elk, a Taos Pueblo man who attended Carlisle for seven years beginning in 1883. The Carlisle rituals he was exposed to became painfully familiar to subsequent ranks of boarding school students. His hair was shorn, he donned a uniform, went to church, eventually conversed in English, and after a while he "began to say Indians were bad" (Embree 1939). When he returned to Taos, now as "Rafael," his schooling was belittled by important elders in the community. He had abandoned his Pueblo education. Rafael left Taos, and did not rejoin the community until his marriage several years later to a young Pueblo woman. Sun Elk's exile was deeply felt, but not permanent.

I came from a family that . . . went to boarding schools, all of them. But my parents never wanted me to go to a boarding school. I used to feel like I was left out . . . and I didn't know a lot of people from the different pueblos because I didn't go to a boarding school.

SHARON DRYFLOWER REYNA, TAOS PUEBLO, BORN 1949 (HEARD MUSEUM 1999)

Sharon Dryflower
Reyna, Taos Pueblo,
1997.

The experiences of later generations of boarding school students suggest an alternative history. The Carlisle experience was radical in 1883, while in later years large numbers of young Indian people were educated in off-reservation boarding schools. Those destined for school often left home with brothers or sisters, cousins and friends. Boarding school students graduated, frequently married classmates, and were welcomed home to reservation communities bustling with boarding school alumni.

Families insisted on keeping in touch with children at school, undaunted by distance and sluggish communication. Countless letters passed between boarding school and home. The best letters informed children of impending visits, holidays at home, or plans for a summer vacation. Letters affirmed that children

were remembered and loved. Basil Johnston, Ojibwe, recalled the significance of letters from home in a poignant and humorous memoir, *Indian School Days:*

> Such a letter gave a boy hope and inspiration and the strength to go on from month to month, from year to year. It was for such a letter that boys with parents who were literate congregated around the prefect at mail call. Orphans and boys whose parents could not write did not bother, and it was easy to tell that they were sad. For those of us from Cape Croker, it was our custom to retire to a corner whenever one of us received a letter, to share the news from home. The recipient first read the letter silently, usually skimming over the news of deaths, births, weddings and other irrelevant news to bore in on the sweet passages that promised "You are coming home." After the silent reading, the lucky recipient read his letter aloud to his compatriots, and then passed it on to his friends. (Johnston 1989)

Graduation, 1968, Phoenix Indian High School, Arizona.

7385 "Mosqui Indians." Chief Lo-Ma-Hung-Yo-Ma, arrested at Oraibi, November 25th and 26th 1894, for seditious conduct and confined at Alcatraz Island, California, since January 3rd, 1895. *Taber* Photo., S.

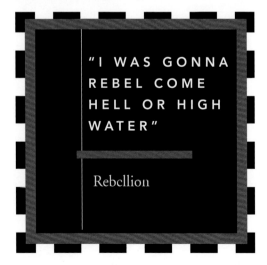

"I WAS GONNA REBEL COME HELL OR HIGH WATER"

Rebellion

BASIL JOHNSTON WROTE THAT HE WAS "SENTENCED" to a Canadian residential school in 1934, where he joined "135 inmates" aged four to sixteen. The Jesuit boarding school he attended was one of seventy-six contemporary institutions that the Canadian government funded to comply with that country's policy of assimilation through Indian education. Small rebellions supplied a large arsenal in the daily war against the priests who ran the school. Students dawdled in their tasks, stole food to supplement a diet of mush, smoked cigarettes, and played pranks. Johnston wrote, "the total sum of our ambitions" was to be "rescued or released" and "restored to our families and homes" (Johnston 1989).

Curtis Thorpe Carr, Creek, a student at Chilocco 1927–1935, recalled similar mischief:

> I wasn't really a mean kid. I got into a lot of mischief and most kids did there, there's no other way you could *survive....* Any time you take a bunch of kids and you put 'em together in that kind of environment and you try to control their thoughts and what they do and everything, it's impossible! ... We used to *deliberately* do things just to show them that we could do it and get away with it. ... I happened to be one that ... couldn't stand somebody telling me what to do every minute of the day or night. That just went against my nature and everything I believed in, and I was gonna rebel come hell or high water. (Lomawaima 1994)

When friction or homesickness became unbearable, students in every boarding school across Canada and the United States reached the same resolution and ran away. For older students, running away could be a rite of passage after years of repression. A mother from Wisconsin, who learned her son had abandoned school with a group of Oneida and Menominee boys, wrote, "Vernon is quite hard to manage since he got to be older and he does not like his parents to tell him things because he is now 18 yrs. old." Youthful boarding school students, many of them runaways, were likely candidates for further government encounters. In 1919, the Indian Office in Washington telegrammed their concern: "Naval Department in Kansas City continues to enlist Haskell deserters although we have written them vigorously. Will you take up with headquarters?"

Safety was foremost in the minds of parents when children ran away from school. Adolescent runaways were often oblivious to the dangers of winter weather and other hazards of the open road. One historian has uncovered tragic results for students who ran away from the Rapid City Indian School to Pine Ridge

Facing: "Mosqui Indians," Alcatraz, 1895. Students in the boarding schools were not the only ones to resist federal educational policies; parents also resisted by trying to keep their children at home. In 1895, Chief Lomahogyniomi and eighteen other Hopi men from the village of Oraibi were incarcerated at Alcatraz because of their resistance, including refusing to enroll their children in federal schools. They were imprisoned from January until August (James 1974).

Curtis Thorpe Carr, Creek, and his wife Marilyn Carr, 1993.

Dear Dad, I suppose you will be surprised to know that I am here. I know I have made a big mistake and it is hard for me to think of the grief it will cause you Dad. Dad I was discouraged I just went mad. I realize what I have done and am very sorry. I'll go back next year and like it.

FLANDREAU RUNAWAY, 1931 (CHILD 1998)

[48]

in 1909. In a nine-day December sojourn, two young boys arrived with frostbite so severe their legs had to be amputated below the knee. A year later two Rapid City School runaways were killed by a train after the exhausted boys fell asleep on the tracks. They were part of a group of six headed home for a tribal celebration (Riney 1999).

"Running away" took many different forms. Students managed to find private space within the regimented lives and ordered spaces of boarding school campuses. Private spaces were well-guarded retreats from the constant surveillance of adult staff and teachers. At Chilocco Indian School in the 1930s, boys had the run of eight thousand acres, and they built gang hideouts, as well as more individual refuges, in the catalpa groves used to grow fence posts.

Curtis Thorpe Carr recalled students' time in the spaces they created: "They'd have stomp dances out at night, in the early years. They'd go out and build a fire, and parch corn . . . and it was a lot of fun" (Lomawaima 1994). The "parched corn" societies at Chilocco and the stomp dances held by boys of the southeastern tribes were an important component of the social

We even built little dugouts along some of the steep creek banks where the water didn't come up anymore, dig out a place and put a roof over it and sod it, and have a little place we could go on our own. Even one year . . . we built a little shack, put a tin roof on it . . . had a little potbellied wood burning stove in there, and go down there in the wintertime and crack walnuts and sit in the warm shack. . . . Those things I remember with great fondness.

CURTIS THORPE CARR, CREEK, (LOMAWAIMA 1994)

life that was created by students in private spaces. Students were resourceful and ingenious—they found ways and means, times and places, to speak their own languages, eat their own foods, and exercise religious practices. Girls were generally much more closely watched than the boys, but they also managed to smuggle bean sandwiches out of the kitchen, tell stories after lights out, even hold peyote meetings in their dorm rooms. Private moments knitted students together in shared joy, shared language, or shared mischief.

Time at school varied from student to student. Some students ran away or happily gave in to the wishes of lonesome parents, but most stayed for a full term of study. After leaving, some entered the military, while others found jobs, married classmates, or migrated home.

INDIAN BOARDING SCHOOL:
THE RUNAWAYS

BY LOUISE ERDRICH

Home's the place we head for in our sleep.
Boxcars stumbling north in dreams
don't wait for us. We catch them on the run.
The rails, old lacerations that we love,
shoot parallel across the face and break
just under Turtle Mountains. Riding scars
you can't get lost. Home is the place they cross.

The lame guard strikes a match and makes the dark
less tolerant. We watch through cracks in boards
as the land starts rolling, rolling till it hurts
to be here, cold in regulation clothes.
We know the sheriff's waiting at midrun
to take us back. His car is dumb and warm.
The highway doesn't rock, it only hums
like a wing of long insults. The worn-down welts
of ancient punishments lead back and forth.

All runaways wear dresses, long green ones,
the color you would think shame was. We scrub
the sidewalks down because it's shameful work.
Our brushes cut the stone in watered arcs
and in the soak frail outlines shiver clear
a moment, things us kids pressed on the dark
face before it hardened, pale, remembering
delicate old injuries, the spines of names and leaves.

At the beginning of the twentieth century, social engineers believed that appropriate architectural forms could contribute to the "civilizing" process, and federal school planners deliberately chose a style of institutional architecture that would impress and uplift students. Grand physical plants on boarding school campuses served two purposes: They stood as symbols to the surrounding American society of the "good works" undertaken by the government's Indian Service, and they were designed to shape the tastes and values of Indian students. By some mysterious alchemy, large, multi-story buildings supposedly would transform students living within their spaces.

When a new dormitory for Indian girls was completed at an eastern school in 1882, a teacher described for the school newspaper the residents' first evening in the home: "Darkness and silence fell upon the building, clouds of mist and rain shut it in, but angel wardens seemed to guard it and make it light and musical. . . . Years of instruction could not do for the Indian girls what a building of their own had accomplished immediately" *(Southern Workman* November 1882).

Boarding schools segmented and organized spaces, inside and outside of buildings. The separation of spaces by function is a powerful symbol of civilized living in American domestic architecture—for every space a function, and for every function a space. It is easy to see the results of this thinking in the American homes of the last century. Families and architects have come to agree on the necessity of separate spaces for children (nurseries, play rooms, rec rooms, and private bedrooms); for cooking and food serving (kitchens, pantries, "formal" dining rooms, breakfast nooks, and barbecue areas); for sleeping and individual privacy (a bedroom for each family member); and various specialized activities (den, home office, workshop, sewing room, TV room, and most recently, home entertainment center). Boarding school students were taught explicit rules, such as "food must never be kept in a room where people sleep" (Reel 1901). Outside spaces were clearly marked off by picket fences, sidewalks that led nowhere, pruned trees, and neatly grassed yards.

—LOMAWAIMA

I am very thankful to you people for all good you have taught my daughter while she was in school and that **she is a graduate girl now.** I am proud of her. I am sorry I can't be there on the Graduating exercise oh I would like to have been there. When will you send the Oneidas home? Let me know so I will know where to meet my daughter.

Office and entrance to Haskell Institute, Lawrence, Kansas, early 1900s.

Oh yes, [lights out came] very early. But we didn't have any screens on the windows and bugs would fly in. Sometimes we'd catch a junebug . . . and tie paper under its legs, little pieces of paper, watch 'em fly around. Oh, it was fun, [we] entertained ourselves!

POTAWATOMIE WOMAN, ENTERED CHILOCCO 1923

(LOMAWAIMA 1994)

For parents, the return of children was long-awaited, happy, and celebrated. They wrote to boarding schools to make plans for the upcoming train passage, send money to children if need be, or simply to remark on past accomplishments and express gratitude.

Students, on the other hand, may have been surprised at how leaving school evoked a complex range of emotions. Basil Johnston captured this moment of parting:

The ones staying behind tried to make light of the parting, but it was not an easy thing to say goodbye to friends who had shared a brotherhood and sustained one another through periods of dejection over the two, three, four, five and six years past. For those leaving and saying farewell it was easily the happiest occasion, and "Farewell" was uttered without regret. But it was not an easy thing for the boys left behind to see this bond, formed out of the dissolution of families, broken. For them, saying good-bye was a re-enactment of the day the bond with mothers and fathers and grandparents, brothers and sisters and homes was sundered with "Goodbye." (Johnston 1989)

Alphonse Caswell, Red Lake Ojibwe, and Ethelbert Branchaud Caswell, White Earth Ojibwe, ca. 1940. The seeds for many unions were planted in government boarding schools. "Al" and "Bert" met as teenagers when he was a student at Flandreau and she lived across the Minnesota border, attending the Pipestone school. The proximity of the two schools allowed many opportunities for students from one to meet students from the other; for Al and Bert a fortuitous introduction led to half a century of successful marriage. The first years of their relationship were difficult. Al's parents had died, he had two younger siblings to consider, and the Great Depression had descended over the Great Lakes. A post-graduation job watching for forest fires at Red Lake as part of the WPA helped them along their way.

ORA PRO NOBIS (PRAY FOR US)

BY OSKINIKO LARRY LOYIE

Excerpt from Act One, Scene 1.1: The Meeting

GEORGE *laughs:* Don't eat the pencils! *Shakes his head, addresses audience.* Some people just don't get it.

He looks thoughtful. Hector's comment brings up memories from the past. To audience. When I entered the residential school for the first time, I remember I did everything I was told to do. If I didn't, the ever-present yanking of my hair, a pinched cheek or a slug on the head with a ring of keys kept me in line. As time went on, I didn't want to be good. I tried to break every rule but not get caught of course.

Like the time I found the priest's gun hidden in his room and snuck it out to the ice house to show my pals. There was one big block of ice out there. I lifted the gun to pretend to shoot. Bang! Somehow it went off. But no one came. Lucky that time.

Looking back on residential school, I know now that I must have been good. After all, I didn't get a beating that often.

Excerpt from Act Two, Scene 2.6: The Knife

Recess. Music is youthful but sad. John, Joseph, George, Raymond and Sniffer sit on the sidewalk of the school. Isaac practices Knife.

ISAAC: Yes. I'm going to run away. It's too lonesome for me here. I have to do something.

GEORGE: Where would you go? How would you get home?

ISAAC: I ain't going home. I'm gonna be an outlaw! I can steal some horses, Father's gun and some food, and head over the mountains to Texas. I'll capture the Father and the Sisters and tie them up and leave 'em with the Indians! Then I would buy a big ranch and take you guys away from here. Why, I might even be a big hero or even a movie star.

YMCA, Carlisle Indian
School, 1884.

PART TWO

"THE HONEST FACTS CONCERNING MY RACE"

LIFE BEYOND SCHOOL

String ensemble, Carlisle
Indian School, Pennsylvania,
ca. 1890.

INTRODUCTION

K. TSIANINA LOMAWAIMA

BOARDING SCHOOLS WERE DESIGNED to create a new kind of American Indian person: detribalized, fluent and literate in English, economically self-sufficient, hard-working, and self-disciplined. The schools' academic curriculum, trades and domestic training, military discipline, and regimentation of student life all fit together to achieve these federal goals. As we have seen in the first part of this book, Indian students and Indian parents brought their own intentions, plans, and hopes into the boarding school system and influenced the institutions that had been created to transform them. Bureaucratic indifference triggered parental outcries; discipline triggered student resistance; and regimentation triggered rebellion. Over many difficult decades, Indian people forged an intense and meaningful relationship with the boarding school

None at Flandreau understood the role of culture in learning. . . . [A]s I look back it's amazing how the kids persevered and did become successful in life when that component of their life was disregarded so completely in the curriculum.

J. C. WADE, BORN 1938, FLANDREAU SANTEE SIOUX,
TAUGHT AT FLANDREAU 1961—1964 (HEARD MUSEUM 1999)

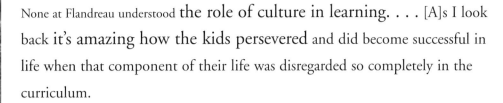

"Indians of the Past" and "Indians of the Present" parade floats, Haskell Institute, Lawrence, Kansas, 1920.

system. "Life at School" was complex and challenging: sometimes demeaning, sometimes joyful. In Basil Johnston's words, students took what little there was and made something better of it.

The kind of complete transformation of American Indian people envisioned by federal policymakers required much more than academic and vocational training. The head and the hands might be retrained in boarding schools, but for "civilization" to really take hold in Native communities, the Native heart had to be remade as well. Federal policymakers were quite conscious of the challenges of emotionally attracting Indian students to "civilized" artistry and music. The schools used art, music, sports, pageants, and displays to inculcate patriotism and a national—not tribal—identity. The schools built "model homes" to house "model families," where parents could be exposed to "civilized" standards of familial affection and love.

I suppose the end to be gained, however far away it might be, is the complete civilization of the Indian and his absorption into our national life, with all the rights and privileges guaranteed to every other individual, the Indian to lose his identity as such, to give up his tribal relations and to be made to feel that he is an American citizen.

RICHARD HENRY PRATT (UTLEY 1964)

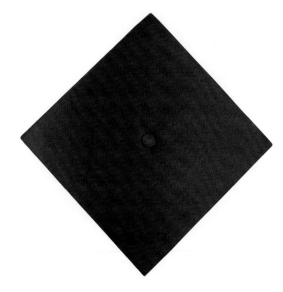

Mortarboard and graduation gown, Phoenix Indian High School, ca. 1980.

In some ways, the programs designed to engage the Native heart were successful. Students learned the violin, and sometimes the jazz trombone; they learned to paint and draw and design; they excelled on football fields and in track arenas. Once again, however, Indian students took federal goals and made something different of them. Student clubs and pageants provided training in oratory that politically active graduates used to advocate for Indian rights. Singers, musicians, and speechmakers came out of the boarding schools and created new opportunities for themselves in the larger world. Kiutus Tecumseh, Yacama, a World War I veteran and boarding school alum, toured the U.S. as a tenor soloist in the 1920s and 1930s. In 1930, he told one of his audiences, "It is my aim to place before the American people the honest facts concerning my race" (Troutman 1999b).

The essays that follow trace the emotional and cultural education that took place within the boarding schools in music rooms, art studios, on athletic playing fields, and within "model families." You will also see how life within the schools was connected to life in Indian communities on and off the reservations. Students returned home—or not—after life at school ended.

There once did live an Indian youth

His tribe Chey-Sioux-Chip-Pot-Jo

His Uncle Sam said—which was the truth,

"To school you ought to go, LO"

So he left the reservation

Left it far behind

Came to seek an education

To soothe his savage mind

Learned how to cultivate the land;

Learned how to keep accounts correctly,

Head applied to hand.

There also lived an Indian maid

Her tribe O-winne-paw-pa;

Her Uncle Sam said, and was obeyed,

"To School, my Minnehaha."

So she left the reservation

Left it far behind

Came to seek an education

To Soothe her savage mind

Came to study at Chilocco

Learned to sew and bake good bread

Learned to keep a home in order

Hands controlled by head.

(1906 school song from the *Chilocco Indian School Journal* 1938)

Philip and Minnie Stabler returned home to the Omaha reservation and built the kind of "civilized home" that their teachers at Hampton Institute dreamed of. Noah and Lucy La Flesche also returned home to the Omaha Agency, but kept up the Omaha songs and dances through the Standing Hawk Lodge. Angel de Cora worked as a designer in New York, Russell "Big Chief" Moore toured with the Lionel Hampton and Louis Armstrong jazz bands, Gertrude Bonnin spoke on the public lecture circuit, and Jim Thorpe and Lewis Tewanima competed in the Olympics. The following essays continue the story of the boarding schools, and the stories of what Indian people made of their lives in school, and their lives beyond school. ⌒

Rayna Green
John Troutman

"BY THE WATERS OF THE MINNEHAHA"

Music and Dance, Pageants and Princesses

Dennison Wheelock, Oneida, band leader at Carlisle Indian School, Pennsylvania, 1890.

THE FOUNDERS OF THE INDIAN SCHOOLS were, from the outset, simultaneously impressed with and horrified by the power and place of song, dance, and ceremonial activities in the lives of Indian people. They quickly learned, perhaps the hard way, that any attempt to "civilize" Indians had to replace "heathen" pleasures, which endangered the assimilative and Americanizing goals of the schools, with equally compelling practices and pastimes. An unrelentingly grim life filled with offprayer, plow, and pen was a life that Indian students, often recruited to mission and federal schools at the point of a gun, hated and rejected.

Although some schools remained grim, permitting neither savage songs nor piano solos in their halls during their relatively short tenure in Indian Country, most schools filled students' minds and mouths with new songs and fitted their hands to different drums—as well as to the plow. Extracurricular programs such as pageants, bands, choirs, and clubs fulfilled the goals of federal Indian policy. They celebrated American patriotism, reinforced Anglo-European social customs and artistic sensibilities, and erased Native culture and history from students' memory, at least in theory. Boarding school clubs, bands, and drill groups socialized students into a world that rejected, or often romanticized, the Indians' past, and sought to Americanize their present.

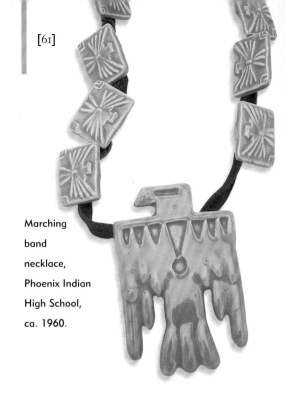

[61]

Marching band necklace, Phoenix Indian High School, ca. 1960.

As with many schemes to eradicate Native traditions in the boarding schools, these attempts to eliminate Indianness backfired. Schools that sought to eradicate the students' traditions and expressions instead provided many Native students with an unusual training ground. Students encouraged to forgo or reject Native gatherings and entertainment now took up the forms of gatherings and entertainment deemed acceptable by the school administrators, putting them to their own social, political, economic, and even religious uses.

Most immigrants in American schools in the latter part of the nineteenth century were given new stories to replace their

Revolutionary War school play, U.S. Indian School, Fort Totten, North Dakota, 1909.

cultures' traditional ones, and Indian students were no exception. These stories served to Americanize Indians, to force them into sharing a partly invented mutual history and culture. The invented stories that became central to the new American mythology—the saga of Hiawatha (Minnehaha and Nokomis), Pocahontas saving Captain John Smith, George Washington and the cherry tree, Squanto and the Pilgrims—were dramatized by Indian students just as they were dramatized by Italian, German, and Eastern European students in schools in New York and Boston in the early part of the twentieth century (Green 1994). The dramas and vignettes, parade floats and oratorical presentations dramatized American myths about Indian dispos-

Columbia's Roll Call, 1892. This pageant was presented before Senator Henry L. Dawes and other visitors on Indian Citizenship Day. Back row, left to right: Frank Bazhaw, Pottawatomie, as Captain John Smith; Ebnezer Kingsley, Winnebago, as John Eliot; William Moore, Sac and Fox, as the Herald of Fame; Frank Hubbard, Penobscot, as George Washington; Adam Metoxen, Oneida, as William Penn; Joseph Redhorse, Sioux, as Taminend, a friend of William Penn. Middle row, left to right: Harry Kingman, Sioux, as the White Mingo, a friend of Kenernal Washington; Laura Face, Sioux, as Pocahontas; James Enouff, Pottawatomie, as Columbus; Juanita Espinosa, Piegan, as Columbia; Addie Stevens, Winnebago, as pilgrim Priscilla Alden; Lucy Trudell, Sioux, as a Quakeress. Front row, left to right: Thomas Last, Sioux, as Samoset; David Hill, Onondaga, as Miles Standish.

session and conquest, with Indian students playing out all the roles of the colonized and colonizers (Green 1989).

Similarly, students were taught "safer," more American forms of music than the music that pervaded life on the reservation. They were instructed to sing in a Western, classical style and to play the piano and brass, string, and woodwind instruments. The orchestral flute replaced the indigenous reed or cedar flute, military bass and snare drums replaced Indian hand drums and water drums, and the violin replaced the fiddle that many had learned to play from the Scots and French a century before.

As students learned music, traditions, and mythological histories from schoolteachers, they also learned new forms of musical and cultural expression from their peers. The schools were filled with Native students from reservations all across the country and inadvertently served as hotbeds of new and foreign Native customs, songs, dances, and traditions that students could adapt and bring back to their home reservations. Of course, during this period students could face severe punishment for expressing tribal customs at school, but they quickly learned strategies to evade or occasionally close the watchful eyes of boarding school matrons and superintendents (Lomawaima 1994; Child 1998).

Music pervaded boarding school campuses. Boarding schools were organized along military lines, and so it was quite natural that their music programs took the form of marching bands that accompanied the uniformed student bodies in marches, drills, and parades. As the talents of the students in these bands and choral groups were honed and recognized, the organizations transcended their original goals of imposing martial order on "undisciplined" Indians.

Patriotic pageant, Sherman Indian School, Riverside, California, n.d.

Name **Frank David Blackhoop**

At Hampton				1912-1919		Diploma
Class	I J. 7	Prep.	I Acad. Nor.	2 Business	2 Business	4 Business
" record	3 - to S.	Fair to good acctg. & spell. r.q. a good mind.	Fair to Good Accts. V.g. Difficult with grammar	Fair. Eng. + Lit. P to S. Type. S to S+ Book S to V.g.	C. Lit. B to C. Econ. B. Sen.Sci. C to D. J.M. Type.	Collecter ity C. Type. C Book D
Trade	-	-	-	-	Very good	-
" record	-	-	M. J. - 9 to Vg	-	-	-
Work	Steamfitting					Janitor
" record	Good +					B -
Church attended	School	Same	Same	Same	Same	Same
Sunday school teacher	Miss Weston	Mr. Crouse	"	Capt. W R Brown	Mr. Edling Late to arrive	Dr. Greg R.O.J.C.
Military rank	Private	Band	Chief Musician	Chief Musician	Band private	Bandlead
Conduct	Good	Good	Good	Good	Very good	Good
Character	"	"	"	"	"	"
General health	"	"		"	Very good	B
Height and weight	149 lbs.					
Sight and hearing	S, glasses.	S. J.	S P.	S. P.	S P.	S P.
Characteristics						
Outing with	Campaign Hampton	J.J. Kidder,	Same	Hampton at home	Hampton	-
" at	2 mos. each	Lake Minnewaska 3 mos	"	-	-	-
Time and wages	$1 per day	$30 per mo.	3 mos. @ $45	-	-	-
Record made	Good Per.	Good.	Good.	Good	Very good	-
Academic scholarship	Rosamund Freeman	Same	Same.	Same	Same	Same
Industrial "	"	"	"	"	"	"
Promoted to	Jun.	Acad. Nor. 1	Acad. Nor. 2	2 Bus. - Alg. + Type. Bkk.	3 Bus +	

Official Student Record, Frank David Blackhoop, Lakota, Hampton Indian School, 1915–1921

FRANK DAVID BLACKHOOP

Frank David Blackhoop/He-we-ta-te/Wind on the Forehead, Standing Rock Lakota, was born June 27, 1897, and attended Hampton from November 4, 1913, until graduation on June 26, 1921. In a letter to Hampton staff dated December 9, 1935, he wrote about his career as a musician and composer:

After I left Hampton Institute in 1922, I became musical director at Santee Normal Training School for Indians in Nebraska. The year following was my desire to study music. I entered Ithaca Conservatory of Music, New York, where I won a scholarship. Later I transferred my credit to American Conservatory in Chicago. Upon leaving this school I was given the position as director of music and bandmaster in the United States Indian Department, first at Chilocco and then at Phoenix, Arizona, and my services terminated at Sherman Institute, Riverside, California, this year upon my resignation.

My present endeavor points to a constructive work that I have had in mind for years, composing Indian tribal melodies and lecture-recital of the Indian and his music. While my compositions are still in manuscripts I hope that in the near future they will find themselves in the repertoire of music halls. Many of these compositions have been played by Indian school bands and army bands now. The best military march was dedicated to our present commissioner of Indian affairs, John Collier, "United States Indian School Band." (Blackhoop 1935) —ARCHULETA

Blackhoop, Frank David   Tribe Sioux   Agency Standing Rock, N.D.

an name He-we-ta-te = Wind on the forehead { Came Nov. 4-1915-   Nov. 21-'18.

19   Born June 27-'97 at Cannon Ball   { with alone   alone

dian Benedict Blackhoop (Father)   { Left Sep. 25-1918   June 26-1921
    Cannon Ball,
dian's address Shields, N.D.   { for Called by Local Board.   Graduation.

r living with mother Yes   Died   of   Mother living   Died   of

r's name and occupation Benedict Blackhoop, Congl.   Mother's name and occupation Agnes
    missionary

ather's race Sioux   ; mother's Sioux   Her father's race Sioux   ; mother's Sioux

Names and Ages		Educated at		Occupation	
Thomas	8	Day School, Shields			
Asa	5				
Mabel	2				

'15-

y supported by   rations 0   annuity $0   rents $17.60 sales $0   labor $
    Sioux benefits when of age   grazing only

owned by		farming	grazing	timber	irrigated by	leased	rates per A	hay cut for	land fenced	cultivated	prin. crop	garde
guardian	640 A	640 A	0	0	Creek	0	$/ -	20 loads	No	40 A	Corn & potatoes	Veg
self	160 A	160 A	0	A	"	0	$ -	0		0 A		

owned by		stories	rooms	sides	roof	floor	well		wagons	location		
guardian		1	2	Log & frame	Shingle	Board	"		1	Cannon Ball.		
self	0											

etc. owned by		barns for	sides	roof	sheds for	horses	cattle	milch cows	hogs	sheep	poultry	farm mac
guardian		6	Log	Sod	Wagon	6	? (range)	1	0	0	Chickens	Plow, c tor, m
self												

s education at { Cannon Ball Day School   8 years
    Fort Yates Boarding School   2 "   '20   Trade
    Santee - finished 8" grade   3 "   Printing.
    farming   at home
s occupation painting   agency   1mo. $1.60 per day
    printing   where "   how long 1 wk.   earned $2.00 "

Congregational   baptized Yes.   joined No. School Church, May 2-1920

at Hampton, past Robt. Higheagle   ; present 0

d to come by Dr. Riggs.   '21   Purpose after leaving Farm

t to learn Did want to be a printer, now want farming.

Marching band jacket, front and back, Flandreau Indian School, South Dakota, ca. 1970.

I got started with the band here under Mr. Robertson (a Sioux instructor), and I guess I was an adept pupil. Mr. Robertson, he played with the Santa Fe City Band downtown. So one summer, just about the time school was out, they needed a couple of E-flat alto horns with that band. So he approached my brother and me. We did real well with the city band.

APACHE STUDENT AT SANTA FE INDIAN SCHOOL, 1928 (HYER 1990)

Students formed numerous music clubs and groups, and school musicians became popular entertainers for fairs and events in the surrounding communities. They were popular not only because of their talents, but, to the consternation of many boarding school officials, because of their exotic appeal to non-Indians, due at least in part to the "Indianist" compositions that were circulating in American popular music.

American Indians had entered the world of popular music in the United States in the late 1800s as subjects of popularized, sanitized, and stereotyped Indian-themed songs by non-Indian composers. Early musicologists transcribed melodies from Indian songs in the nineteenth century, and "Indianist" composers

Facing: Phoenix Indian School band, ca. 1895.

Below: Shawnee Indian School drum and brass band, ca. 1902. Back row, left to right: Frank Purely, Reuben Wolf, Phillip Roubideaux, Richard Shonotowe, Maxie Frizzlehead.

Middle row, left to right: George Pancake, Clay Brown, John Rush, Archie Wells, Lee Daily. Front row, left to right: Moses Crow, John Kimble, Louie McDonald, Perry Farazier.

Haskell
Institute band,
ca. 1905.

Carlisle Indian School dress parade with school band, 1880. Mrs. Walter Baker of the Baker Chocolate Factory endowed Carlisle with the instruments to form a band, and within three months, the group was taking part in evening dress parades with the student body. The band went to the Chicago World's Fair and the Columbian Exposition Parade in New York City, and traveled the United States and Europe performing in concerts and parades.

integrated these melodies into arrangements for orchestras and singers. Songs such as "Hiawatha's Love Melody," "By the Waters of the Minnehaha," and "Indian Love Call" became as popular in boarding school classrooms as they were on the American stage. These songs praised a romanticized ideal of Native identity, the tribal version of which school officials had tried for years to eradicate. Songs evoked popular romanticized images such as the Indian maiden and the noble savage (Green 1975, 1994), but were seen as benign by school officials because they were performed in a non-Indian, and thus "civilized," musical style, negating any of the harmful elements of Indianness that the songs might celebrate.

Music had always been a source of contention between American Indians and the religious and government entities that sought to assimilate them. Before the turn of the century, missionaries and Office of Indian Affairs (OIA) agents struggled to control religious practice and the songs and dances that accompany it by suppressing the Sun Dance and the Ghost Dance, and by restricting "heathen" musical and cultural expression deemed inimical to the goals of Christianization and assimilation. During and after World War I, as boarding school students

"Haskell March" sheet music, 1906.

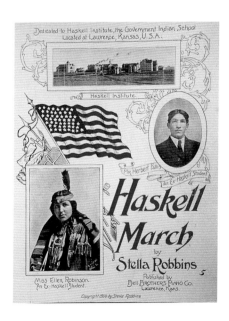

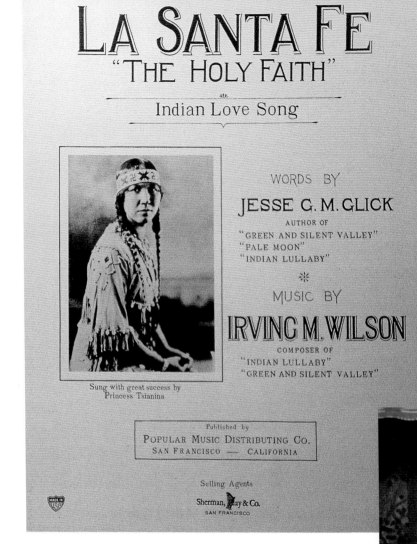

"Land of My Prairie Dreams" sheet music, by Kiutus Tecumseh, 1926, and "La Santa Fe (The Holy Faith, Indian Love Song)" sheet music, 1926.

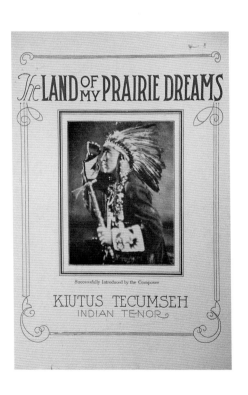

learned new songs and styles, the controversy over music grew in Indian country. American Indians on reservations revived older tribal dances and created new ones (Lomawaima n.d.). In response, missionaries and OIA agents mobilized to stamp out the "dangerous" dances (Troutman 1999a).

On February 23, 1923, Commissioner of Indian Affairs Charles Burke issued a letter addressed "To All Indians," warning them against performing several of their dances on the reservations. Except for certain "decent amusements or occasional feast dances," Indians were instructed not to hold dances unless approved by their OIA reservation superintendents. Burke condemned the performance of any Native dance by children in the schools, and felt that, for a "healthy substitute," they should learn nicer, white dances such as the Maypole Dance, then already prevalent in the schools (Burke 1923). The Native students working in the print shop at Chilocco Indian Agricultural School printed 15,000 of Burke's "Dance Circulars," which were distributed to reservations throughout the country (Blair 1923).

Girls' drill team,
U.S. Indian
School, Fort
Totten, North
Dakota, n.d.

Haskell
students in a
production of
"Hiawatha,"
1922.

Missionaries and OIA agents felt that they were losing control of the very Indian people who earlier would have been considered the success stories of their educational programs. Students who returned home and stepped back into tribal life were said to have gone "back to the blanket." So-called "blanket Indians" disturbed federal officials and even fellow boarding school alumni.

A good many of my brothers and friends have been to school. I teach them that they must not go back to the blanket but on the Rosebud Reservation all the returned Carlyle students have returned to blankets. They are the cause of a great deal of this trouble. [I went to a dance at Black Pike] and saw a number of men who had on war bonets and there was one young man there dressed just like the old men and this man came near and I seen that this young man had a mustache on—it looked so funny. And I was ashamed of myself. I felt so ashamed of myself. He talked better English than I do and I was ashamed. The outward look of him was more like a white man. He spoke the English language and yet he was all painted up. And so there is a great problem. — Dallas Shaw, Lakota (Sioux) missionary, 1922. (Shaw 1922)

Young World War I Indian veterans and boarding school students (such as the young "painted up" Lakota man who spoke better English than Dallas Shaw) were rejuvenating public dances and the fears of local officials. They helped to revitalize the old, forbidden dances, and they also took advantage of a wider pub-

KIUTUS TECUMSEH

Kiutus Tecumseh (born Herman Roberts), Yacama, a World War I veteran, began touring the United States as a tenor soloist around 1924. Tecumseh corresponded and met with Commissioner of Indian Affairs Charles Burke frequently, to discuss the work (or lack thereof) that the OIA was doing for American Indians. Tecumseh attracted audiences with his "authenticity" and novelty, and he encouraged his audiences to reconsider current federal Indian policies and some Indian stereotypes while, like Tsianina Redfeather and other touring musicians, he inadvertently preserved or reinforced others. At a typical performance in 1930, Tecumseh said, "I have been making these talks over the radio in connection with my singing in an effort to better acquaint the public with Indian questions. It is my aim to place before the American people the honest facts concerning my race." He continued, "I am making every effort so that our boys and girls are given a fair chance to attend not only grade and high schools, but colleges as well." While keeping a busy road schedule, he felt duty-bound to visit Indian schools along the way in order to serve as a role model for the students. Tecumseh performed often on the radio, and he also sponsored radio appearances by other Indian singers and performers, such as a group of Haskell students that traveled to Chicago to sing in 1926 (Troutman 1999b). —GREEN AND TROUTMAN

Kansas University
Band Day at
American Royal
Parade, Lawrence,
Kansas, ca. 1940.

The Indian Club,
Haskell Institute,
ca. 1930–1940.

lic interest in American Indian arts. Native dances and performances were held off the reservations for the non-Indian public.
Indians became tourist attractions for non-Natives seeking to
fulfill their frontier fantasies of romanticized Indians dressed in
feathers and immersed in exotic dance.

The Office of Indian Affairs faced an uphill battle trying to
control the music and cultural displays of Native people.
Resistance came from Indians as well as from a burgeoning popular culture that appropriated Indian images, music, and cultural displays (however stereotypical or contrived) to suit their own
purposes. "Indianness" became more lucrative than virtually any
government assimilation program that Indians could adopt. As a
paying proposition, Indianness challenged the assimilationists'
assumption that Indian identity was antithetical to full participation in the American market economy.

Student participation in "Indian" performances demonstrat-
ed to federal officials the failure of their educational program.
They had tried to assimilate children through the schools' coer-
cive programs, designed to break tribal ties and eradicate Native
customs. Indians were finding greater economic security by cel-

I don't think I appreciated my Indianness until I . . . became a senior in high school, when we had our Indian Club here, and I **joined the Indian Club.**

<small>SAN JUAN PUEBLO STUDENT AT SANTA FE INDIAN SCHOOL, 1927 (HYER 1990)</small>

We could use their Indianness to develop the self-esteem. . . . [T]hey had to do research on their background, on their tribal heritage, on their dress. It was interesting for me to learn that many of them did not know their tribal background. They had to work hard.

<small>GEORGIANA DAVENPORT, born 1935 SAC AND FOX, TAUGHT AT PHOENIX INDIAN SCHOOL AND DIRECTED PAGEANTS 1958—1980 (HEARD MUSEUM 1999)</small>

ebrating Indian traditions through music and dance than by taking up individual homesteads and breaking tribal ties. Federal agents were unable to appreciate or even recognize the irony, and they maintained their opposition to "dangerous" Indian dances and music (Troutman 1999a).

Native students and communities, on and off reservations, learned to handle federal anxieties, fears, and repression by creatively disguising their dances and cultural traditions as American patriotic displays. Having learned in the schools that publicly displaying Indianness while promoting citizenship was

Indian Club, Haskell Institute, ca. 1940–1950.

Indian Club

The Indian Dance
Club, Haskell
Institute, ca. 1950.

THE INDIAN DANCE CLUB

HASKELL INSTITUTE
Lawrence, Kansas

acceptable to the ever-anxious white man, reservation Indians began to schedule feast days and ceremonials during "American" and "patriotic" holidays and celebrations. A Fourth of July dance was a much safer, if not the safest, form of dancing, because it seemed to laud the goals of "civilization." Literally and figuratively wrapping themselves in the American flag, Indians used the patriotic holidays—the Fourth of July, Memorial Day, and Arbor Day—or celebratory occasions such as Thanksgiving to convince federal agents that they had a just cause to dance (Ellis 1999).

Instilling patriotism in the hearts and minds of the Indians, particularly the boarding school students, had been a goal of federal Indian education from the beginning (Prucha 1990). Although some OIA officials and missionaries were suspicious of the dancers' intentions, their powers to repress were hampered by the patriotic flavor of the dances and the fact that large segments of the non-Indian public supported the festivities. For students who had to spend so much time away from home, the dances often rejuvenated tribal customs and values, and reinforced bonds with their community. The strength of this bond could explain the students' increasing participation in the dances during the years of most severe repression. For these Native students, in fact, the danger of the dances lay in not executing them, in *not* cementing the ties that might erode while they were away from home for so long.

By the late 1920s, the government was forced to admit that the allotment policies of dividing up reservation lands had failed miserably to provide an adequate economic base for Indian communities. It was also time to recognize the error of policies that hoped to eradicate Native traditions and values. New officials in the Bureau of Indian Affairs (formerly the Office of Indian Affairs) sought a new course in policy that emphasized, to an extent, tribal autonomy and self-governance. John Collier, commissioner of the BIA from 1933 to 1945, was fascinated by Native cultures. In the 1920s he had publicly chastised government repression of Indian dances and traditions (Kelly 1983). Once in office, Collier considered abandoning non-Indian music instruction at the schools and focusing instruction solely on what he considered "real" Indian music. In this regard, Collier was inverting the former federal categories of what was considered "safe" and "dangerous."

During Collier's administration, known as the Indian New Deal, the BIA changed course in policy, seeming to turn the tide against federal suppression of Indian arts and traditions. School

The Indian Dance Club, Haskell Institute, ca. 1950.

Gertrude Simmons Bonnin, Lakota, 1898.

clubs and societies performed traditional music and dance. The new "Indian" clubs insisted on presenting and performing Native art, music, dance, and clothing. The clubs furthered pan-Indian, intertribal ties among the students, since students performed the dances and songs of tribes other than their own, and took new songs and dances back to their own communities—not always with the approval of their elders. Students also took these new "Indianized" performances to communities outside Indian Country. At a time when the vocational and domestic instruction in boarding schools was quite limited, and prospects for work off the reservations were not very promising, many Indian

INDIAN HEADLINERS

Tsianina Redfeather (also known as Princess Tsianina and Tsianina Blackstone), a Creek-Cherokee musician widely known in the United States in the early part of the twentieth century, began her musical training at the Eufaula, Oklahoma, Indian Government School. She performed as a soloist with many orchestras and entertained troops during World War I as a member of the American Expeditionary Forces. She toured the United States with her performing partner, composer Charles Wakefield Cadman. Redfeather was even the subject of an opera, *Shanewis (The Robin Woman)*, the first American opera performed at the Metropolitan Opera in New York for more than a single season. When she retired to California, she organized the Foundation for American Indian Education, a local effort to send Indian men and women to colleges in Albuquerque and Phoenix (Troutman 1999b).

Gertrude Simmons Bonnin, (Zitkala-sá), Lakota, attended Quaker Mission School and White's Indiana Manual Labor Institute in Indiana, then Earlham College, where she won prizes in oratory. She taught two years at the Carlisle Indian School. In 1900, as a violin soloist, she toured to the Paris Exposition with the Carlisle band. She wrote pro-Native literature ("Why I Am a Pagan") aimed at reforming federal policy, and rewrote versions of traditional Lakota tales for mainstream publications such as *Harper's Weekly*. She became a noted advocate, lecturer, and activist for Indian reform, and with her husband co-founded the National Congress of American Indians. She used her considerable oratorical, literary, and musical talents to gain a new stage for her political activities on behalf of Indian sovereignty (Fisher 1979).

Jesse Rowlodge "played leads in school dramas, worked in the school's bank office, played in the band and was a member of the football squad" at Haskell Institute ca. 1910. He returned home to become an important political intermediary, a cultural broker for the Oklahoma Cheyennes and Arapahos, and a congressional lobbyist who fought for Indian political interests and advocated for reform of tribal governance (Berthrong 1994).

Russell Moore, the Pima jazzman known as "Big Chief" Moore, graduated in the 1920s from Sherman Institute, where he learned to play trombone and fell in love with jazz. He toured with Lionel Hampton, the Louis Armstrong big bands, and his own "Powwow Jazz Band," making recordings and an international reputation for his music. He went to the Indian schools and home to Gila River many times, trying to interest younger Indians in jazz.

—GREEN AND TROUTMAN

Tsianina
Redfeather, 1924

Homecoming queens, Haskell Institute, ca. 1940.

musicians and dancers took advantage of the public interest in Indianness to make a decent living doing what they loved to do.

Many Indian students took the musical and oratorical skills they had honed in the schools far beyond the campus. A number of early students became professional performers, actors, and musicians on the mainstream stage and in "Indian" performance venues. Many of the "Show" Indians after 1890 performed with the Wild West shows, the circuses, the movies, the tourist circuit—Niagara Falls, Wisconsin Dells, Glacier National Park, Grand Canyon—and the popular stage. They had been at least introduced to "Indian" performance in the boarding schools, and many performers created and refined their arts there. As students, they learned formal dramatic arts from school vignettes and plays, as well as the informal dramatic arts of playing Indian, wearing "citizen" clothes, and traditional Native dress (often not their own)—learning to persuade white folk that they were both Native and civilized (Green 1988; Deloria 1998).

Many of the Indian school clubs in the 1930s were similar to clubs in mainstream American schools, organized to promote citizenship and American values. Around World War II, the Indian school clubs became more like activities in American schools everywhere, yet more and more "Indian" as well. The many Home Economics Clubs, Boy Scout troops, Glee Clubs, 4-H Clubs, Lettermen's Clubs, Key Clubs, Highway Safety Patrol Clubs, Penmanship Clubs, Student Councils, Future Homemakers of America, and Girl Scout "Adventure in Americanism" groups taught civic responsibility and the democratic process. By the 1960s these clubs and societies yielded to other organizations, such as the National Honor Society, computer clubs, Model United Nations, and Future Teachers Clubs, which may say as much about the mainstreaming of Native societies as it does about the mainstreaming of Indian schools. At the same time, during and after the 1960s, Native students, staff, and teachers demanded organizations more culturally and politically attuned to Native issues and concerns. Today on many public and private university campuses one can find Indian clubs and other organizations—inherently both political and cultural—created by and for Indian students.

In addition to music, oratory, and civic and Indian clubs, Princess pageants proliferated within Indian schools and Native communities. The hundreds of Miss Bacones, Miss Chiloccos, and later, Miss Navajos and Miss Cherokees, even Miss Indian Americas—like their performer stage predecessors—were born in the schools, taking their cues from the white society that had long deemed "nice" Indian girls to be princesses (Green 1975).

Felicita Cromwell Cook, White Mountain Apache, Phoenix Indian School All Class Reunion, 1999. In 1990, Cook was the last Miss Phoenix Indian High School.

Santa Fe Indian
School 1953
Homecoming
Chief Simon
Toya, Jemez, and
Homecoming
Princess Dolorita
Esquibel, San
Felipe.

Since the princesses had to make their own costumes, moving
from simple sashes to complete traditional "regalia," the princess
traditions in the schools helped restore traditional knowledge
such as Native language use and Native arts, including bead-
work, leatherwork, and silverwork. Certainly the princess tradition at the schools—which ex-students then took back to their
homes—propped up *both* stereotypical images of Indian women
and the retention, acquisition, and valuing of cultural knowledge
(Green 1975, 1994).

Some students applied the skills they acquired in the schools
within public political forums. They learned the fine arts of
recitation and debate, honing the oratorical skills so valued in
many traditional communities. In the nineteenth century,
Indian school alumni toured the Chautauqua and other lecture
circuits, speaking for Indian reform. Reciting the Declaration of
Independence and Mrs. Browning's sonnets in school evolved

into making speeches exhorting against the Dawes Act and Burke's Dance Circular in the 1920s and 1930s. Though some preached against the traditional pursuits and practices of their people (Coleman 1994), others converted the leadership, music, oratorical skills and repertoires learned in schools to serve Nativist agendas. Just as often, they transferred skills and repertoires learned at the schools into more generalized skills that would earn a living, supplement income, or provide a means of travel away from home.

Debaters, orators, student council leaders, and princesses often became political leaders of their tribes and pueblos; choir and club members became instructors, sometimes in the same Indian schools where they had been students. More recently, in the 1980s and 1990s, a new Native arts movement was spawned by students becoming professional musicians, actors, and writers. Boarding school students learned, in the nineteenth and twentieth centuries, that all the world beyond the school was a stage, and that they could be players on it.

Had the varsity sweaters, tailcoats, violins, and military marches "soothed their savage minds?" Had Euro-American pageantry and music taught students to rule by white heads, not Indian hearts? Students had, in so many respects, learned to play Indian for a white audience, on the one hand, and to play white for their teachers on the other. They were well instructed in the most bourgeois and middle-class of Anglo-American institutions and value systems. But students did learn more than simply a means to please their teachers, government officials, and the white fathers of the towns and communities around them. When we see the evolution of Indian Clubs, over time; what the princess competitions and pageants became; what the music and dance turned into, we can take some comfort—from the past and in the future. In so many ways, Native students turned attempts to repress and replace Native tradition into something viable and vital, for themselves as individuals and for their Native communities, local and national. ⌒

St. John's Episcopal Church Indian Choir, Hampton, Virginia, ca. 1902. Back row, left to right: Unidentified; Joseph Blackhawk, Winnebago; Reverend C. B. Bryan; unidentified. Third row, left to right: Unidentified; Jane S. Worcester, faculty; Isaac N. Webster, Oneida; unidentified. Second row, left to right: Rose Hill, Oneida; three unidentified people. Front row, left to right: Two unidentified people; Josephine Hill, Oneida.

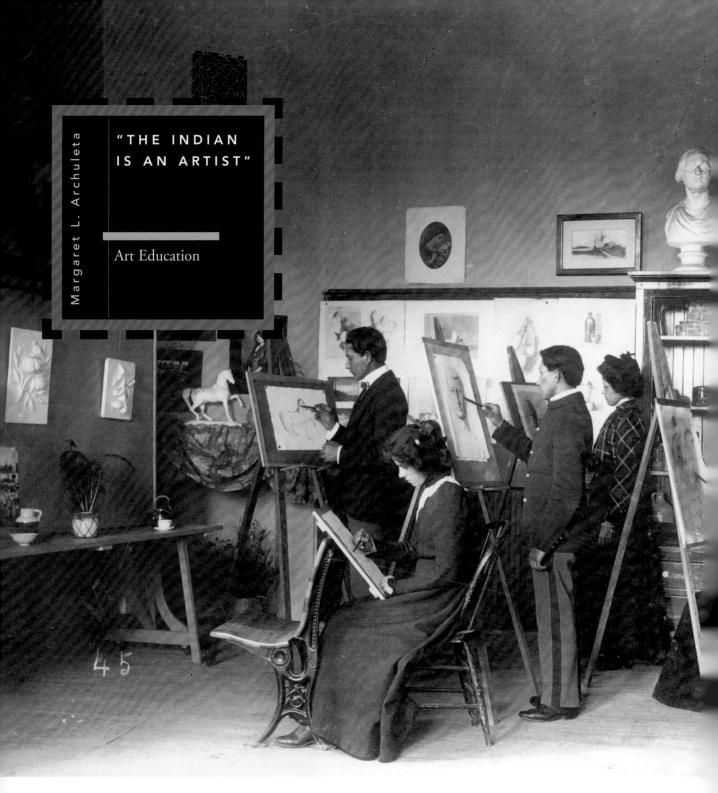

"THE INDIAN IS AN ARTIST"

Art Education

Art class, Carlisle Indian School, Pennsylvania, ca. 1901. Formal easel painting was part of the curriculum prior to 1906.

As with music, art education in Indian boarding schools had the goal of transforming students into model American citizens. Training focused exclusively on studies of European masters while promoting conventional media such as easel painting. In the early twentieth century, reform-minded "friends of the Indian" argued for inclusion of Indian culture in boarding school curricula. Their agenda met with success when President Theodore Roosevelt appointed Francis E. Leupp as commissioner of Indian affairs in 1905. Leupp's appointment

The simple dignity of Indian design lends itself well to ways of conventional art and the American people must . . . give recognition to another phase of the Indian's nature, which is his art.

ANGEL DE CORA, 1909

Leupp Art Studio,
Carlisle Indian
School, Pennsylvania,
ca. 1907.

signaled a move towards incorporating cultural content into the boarding school programs.

Leupp's prior work with the Indian Rights Association had helped him recognize the value of preserving some Native traditions, particularly Indian art and music. He viewed Indians as innately talented people suspended in a less evolved state than Euro-Americans, but fully capable of change and progress. "The Indian is a natural warrior, a natural logician, a natural artist. Our proper work with him [the Indian] is Improvement, not Transformation" (Curtis 1920).

Although at times I yearn to express myself in landscape art, I feel that designing is the best channel in which to convey the native qualities of the Indian's decorative talent.

ANGEL DE CORA, 1911 (MCANULTY 1976)

A year after Leupp's arrival in the Indian office, Angel de Cora, a young Winnebago woman trained in Western fine art, was hired at Carlisle to foster the native talents of the Indian students, marking the first official program for teaching Indian art at the boarding schools. De Cora became one of the most significant Indian artists of her time, though her many contributions to the development and teaching of "Indian art" have been largely overlooked. De Cora was trained at prestigious art schools as an illustrator, painter, and designer by some of the most influential American artists of the time. She became a published writer and active member of the Society of American Indians. Before her untimely death, she was widely regarded as an advocate for not only the appreciation of Indian art but for its acceptance as American art.

The boarding school system was an important influence in de Cora's life even before her arrival at Carlisle. She attended Hampton from 1883 to 1891, where she excelled in both music and art. She graduated from Smith College in 1896, and went on to study art in Philadelphia and at Cowles Art School and the Boston Museum of Fine Arts. Her art education was based in the academic traditions of the time in America: the Barbizon school, American romantic realism, and American impressionism (McAnulty 1976). She was talented, independent, and self-sufficient with an education that provided her with the means to earn a living as an artist. De Cora was a boarding school success story.

In 1902 de Cora moved to New York City, where she opened a studio and supported herself doing portraits and landscape work. She also wrote and illustrated two stories, "The Sick Child" and "Grey Wolf's Daughter," for *Harper's New Monthly Magazine* (published in February and November 1899) and illustrated Francis La Flesche's *The Middle Five: Indian Boys at School,* Mary Catherine Judd's *Wigwam Stories,* Zitkala-Šá's *Old Indian Legends,* and Natalie Curtis's *The Indian Book.* Her primary source of income was illustration.

Facing: Angel de Cora, Winnebago (1871–1919), ca. 1900. De Cora was born on the Winnebago (today the Ho-Chunk) reservation, Dakota County, Nebraska, on May 3, 1871. She was given the name Hinook-Mahiwi-Kilinaka, meaning "Fleecy Cloud Floating in Place" and "Woman Coming on the Clouds of Glory," which was translated into English as "Angel." Her father, David (Tall) de Cora was the fourth son of Little de Cora, who was leader of the Nebraska Winnebagos until his death in 1887. Her mother was from another prominent Winnebago family, the LaMeres.

Two untitled
paintings by Angel
de Cora, ca. 1890,
above, and ca.
1897, right.

Angel de Cora left her successful career as an illustrator when
she accepted the post of art instructor at the Carlisle Indian
School. Her dedication to Indian art led her to the classroom.
She believed it was possible to teach art to boarding school students in a way they had never experienced, saying, "I shall not be
expected to teach in the white man's way, but shall be given complete liberty to develop the art of my own race and to apply this,
as far as possible, to various forms of art, industries and crafts"
(Curtis 1920).

Carlisle's philosophy of assimilation was an obstacle to de Cora. Since its beginning in 1879, the school had discouraged all things Indian, and even the Native students were reluctant to accept the radical change in teaching, or readily embrace the concept of learning Indian art. De Cora recognized the immense task ahead of her:

> An Indian's self-respect is undermined when he is told that his native customs and crafts are no longer of any use because they are the habits and pastimes of the crude man. If he takes up his native crafts he does it with the sense that he has "gone back to barbarism." On taking up the work at Carlisle I found one of the necessary things to do was to impress upon the minds of my pupils that they were Indians, possessing native abilities that had never been recognized in the curriculum of the Government schools. (de Cora 1909)

Natalie Curtis, an advocate for Indian reform who had introduced de Cora to Commissioner Leupp, wrote, "Before Angel de Cora could begin her work the slate had not only to be wiped clean but thrown out the window! [H]er classes were told that they need not copy the teacher, or anybody else. The children were to express themselves. Her manner of teaching was to set her scholars a given task and then leave the room, freeing her pupils from the restraint of the teacher's presence" (Curtis 1920).

In 1897, as a student, de Cora had traveled to the Fort Berthold reservation (home of the Arikaras, Mandans, and Hidatsas), in North Dakota. There she observed the making of cultural items, and noted the use of traditional designs in all aspects of the work. These observations fostered her convictions about Indian art—that art was an inborn talent among all Indians, and that if one could understand the designs that were so natural to Indians, one could begin to understand Indian art as a whole. De Cora's experiences in Indian Country influenced her teaching methodology. In the unlikely setting of Carlisle, she laid out a course of study that examined the styles and designs of each tribe.

> The nature of Indian art is formed on a purely conventional and geometric basis, and our endeavors at the Carlisle Indian School have been to treat it as a conventional system of designing. The Indian pictured the broader aspects of nature in symbolic figures of geometrical shapes with each tribal scheme of symbolisms. The study of the fundamental figures was followed by the combined figures, made up of two or more of the elements of design, complex figures made by

"This department under the new idea of preserving Indian art was started February, 1906. The plan is to encourage the Indian to use the conventional designing that is the characteristic art of his race.

"The day of the ornamental buckskin is past and the tribes that made basket and pottery find little time as they up the commercial strife of the white man, to keep up their native industries. About the only way to perpetuate the use of the Indian designs is to apply them on modern articles of use and ornament that the young Indian is taught to make. In the class they are asked to make designs for rugs, frieze for wall decoration, borders for printing, and designs for embroidery of all kinds. We have just started to apply our designs on basswood articles in color or with the pyro-graphic needle.

"We decorate skins for wall hangings or for the sofa cushions covers. We also use our designs for more serious work. Our chief aim along this method of designing is to work them into rugs. We are using both the Navajo and the Persian methods of weaving. The Persian method allows them more freedom to carry out their intricate designs. The work is slowly but steadily increasing in both interest and importance." (de Cora 1908) —ARCHULETA

repeated use of two or more of the elements of design. Under this analytic system we have studied the various tribal styles. [T]he Indian's art was a well established system of designing and if the young school Indian was permitted to practice it in the class room it would make interesting exhibition . . . and moreover it might be further cultivated by the educated Indians and adapted to modern methods. (de Cora 1911)

To broaden her own education in tribal artistic design, de Cora traveled to New Mexico in 1907 to visit with Pueblo women artists. De Cora understood how important it was to gain insight into Indian women's cultural lives in order to better understand their artistic designs, and her observations and experiences in the pueblos reinforced her belief that design was the foundation of Indian art. A year after her New Mexico sojourn, de Cora married William Lone Star Dietz, a Lakota football star and one of her former Carlisle students. A honeymoon trip to meet new relatives on the Northern Plains turned into another opportunity for de Cora to meet with women artists. There she dispensed practical advice such as the suggestion to do bead-

Facing: Teaching weaving, Carlisle Indian School, Pennsylvania, ca. 1906–1914. De Cora believed that design was the quint-essential aspect of Indian art, and for her classes, she broke down Native designs into their basic elements (note the blackboard) and encouraged her students to use them in their artwork.

Above: Learning to appliqué, Sherman Indian School, Riverside, California, ca. 1950. Note the Native designs the students are using.

work on small pouches that could be sold to tourists as purses, opera bags, or decorative holders for sewing paraphernalia. Encouraging Indian artists to use their designs in a modern context developed into an important teaching theme for de Cora.

> The designs form the nucleus of Native Indian Art. The Indians are gifted in original ideas of ornamentation. To train and develop this decorative instinct of the Indian to modern methods and apply it on up-to-date house furnishings is the nature and intent of the Native Indian Art Department. . . . The Indian designs modified and applied to interior house decoration are especially in harmony with the so-called "mission" style, [and] the geometric designs lend themselves well to the simple and straight lines of mission furniture.
> (de Cora 1911)

De Cora's desire to have Indian designs utilized in a modern context, as in mission-style home decoration, was compatible with Commissioner Leupp's belief in economic self-sufficiency for individual American Indians. Later, in the 1930s, Commissioner of Indian Affairs Collier would support the development of an Indian arts and crafts market as one path to tribal economic development. The results of de Cora's unconventional teaching methods drew the recognition of the Office of Indian Affairs.

Phoenix Indian School dining room china, ca. 1900s. Inca Ware, New Castle, Pennsylvania.

VOLUME 3, NO. 10   JUNE, 1911   A DOLLAR A YEAR

An Illustrated Magazine by Indians

THE RED MAN

Published Monthly by **THE CARLISLE INDIAN PRESS**

UNITED STATES INDIAN SCHOOL, CARLISLE, PENNSYLVANIA

Society of American Indians, Ohio State University, Columbus, Ohio, 1911.

On Columbus Day 1911 a group of Indian intellectuals and scholars gathered at Ohio State University with white progessives to form an Indian national reform organization. First named the American Indian Association, the organization soon changed its name to the Society of American Indians, "A National Organization of Americans." The purpose of the Society was to "work for the uplift and advancement of the American Indian" (Society of American Indians 1913). Founding members included such Indian leaders as Carlos Montezuma, Charles A. Eastman, Sherman Coolidge, Charles E. Daganett, Gertrude Simmons Bonnin, Angel de Cora, Emma D. Johnson Goulette, Marie L.B. Baldwin, Rosa B. La Flesche, and Laura M. Cornelius Kellogg. A number of the founders were former boarding school students.

The society focused on individuals rather than tribes for its membership, and included non-Indians. Membership was divided into five levels: active, for adult persons of Indian blood; Indian associate, for Indians from outside of the United States or persons of Indian blood not on any tribal roll; junior, for Indians under the age of twenty-one; associate, for persons of non-Indian blood interested in Indian welfare; and honorary, for persons of distinguished attainment as elected by the society (Society of American Indians 1916).

As recorded in 1913 in its handbook, the society had seven objects or goals:

First. To promote and co-operate with all efforts looking to the advancement of the Indian in enlightenment which leave him free as a man to develop according to the natural laws of social evolution.

Second. To provide through our open conferences the means for a free discussion on all subjects bearing on the welfare of the race.

Third. To present in a just light the true history of the race, to preserve its records and emulate its distinguishing virtues.

Fourth. To promote citizenship and to obtain the rights thereof.

Fifth. To establish a legal department to investigate Indian problems, and to suggest and to obtain remedies.

Sixth. To exercise the right to oppose any movement that may be detrimental to the race.

Seventh. To direct its energies exclusively to general principles and universal interests, and not allow itself to be used for any personal or private interest. —ARCHULETA

De Cora traveled nationally as a lecturer, giving demonstrations on Indian art to groups such as the National Education Association and the Lake Mohonk Conference, which advocated for Indian reform. In 1911, de Cora was invited to present a keynote speech at the first annual conference of the Society of American Indians, a newly organized advocacy group comprised of educated Indian individuals who supported reform. Angel de Cora and Lone Star Dietz joined Carlos Montezuma, Charles Eastman, and other prominent leaders as founding members of the society.

De Cora left Carlisle in 1915 because of changes in the administration, the departure of Commissioner Leupp, and Dietz's move to Washington state for a new coaching job. She joined Dietz in Washington, but three years later the couple divorced and she returned to New York, taking a job as an illustrator at the New York State Museum in Albany. A year later, in 1919, she died during the great influenza epidemic at the age of

Pottery making, molding and smoothing jars, Phoenix Indian School, Arizona, 1934.

48. Upon learning of Angel de Cora's death, Elaine Goodale Eastman wrote a memoriam for *American Indian Magazine.* "Life is gone," she wrote, "but its inspiration remains. Living, she loved her people; dying, she left them all that she had to give."

De Cora taught at Carlisle for only nine years and transformed the school's approach to art instruction during that time, but her art program at Carlisle ended when she left. It was not until the early 1930s, as a result of the 1928 Meriam Report and the sweeping reforms that followed, that culture-based art programs were reintroduced and reinvented at the boarding schools, and tribal artists began teaching Indian art there. During this time the federal government also began to recognize the potential economic value of the tribal traditional arts for tribes. In 1936 the Indian Arts and Crafts Board was established for the purpose of promoting and protecting the production of Indian art.

Nearly a century after Angel de Cora opened the Department of Indian Art at Carlisle, her contributions to the larger world as an artist and teacher are yet to be recognized. Certainly she was ahead of her time. Many of her teaching philosophies began to be realized during the self-determination era of the 1960s, when culture-based education became a part of the education system for Indian children. However, the issues most important to de Cora's vision—defining Indian art and including it as a part of the larger world of American art—remain a challenge for even the most well-established American Indian artists in today's world.

A lot of the art expressions from my culture were absent [from boarding school]—the singing, the dancing, the ceremonies, the rituals—all of those things were not there. Artwise, what did I do? I was the art editor for the yearbook and so that was my art contribution.

MICHAEL KABOTIE, HOPI, BORN 1942, ATTENDED HASKELL 1959–1961 (HEARD MUSEUM 1999)

Pablita Velarde,
Dorothy Dunn,
and Po-Qui,
October 1963.

THE STUDIO AT SANTA FE INDIAN SCHOOL

In response to the Meriam Report of 1928, attitudes regarding Indian arts and crafts began to change within the Office of Indian Affairs. W. Carson Ryan, director of Indian education, designated the Santa Fe Indian School in New Mexico as the arts and crafts center for the entire Indian boarding system. It became significant in the development of Indian art education.

Dorothy Dunn, a graduate of the Art Institute of Chicago, came to Santa Fe Indian School to develop its art program in 1932. She expanded the arts and crafts courses to include a class in painting and design, which became referred to as "The Studio."

Dunn explained the philosophy of the class as follows: "Because the Santa Fe school believes that American Indian painting has a distinct and an important contribution to make to the art of the world, it encourages and develops only true tribal traditions in its painting classes. No European traditions of painting such as light and shade, perspective, anatomy, the use of models, etc. are taught. Advertising art, cartooning, landscape and portrait painting have no place in the school's courses because they are not in keeping with the precedents of Indian art. . . . Work is developed from memory and from research in authentic records. The media used are watercolors, tempera, oils and native earth colors" (Dunn 1937).

The purpose of the program was "to bring out each individual's own best tendencies, keeping them as pure and original as possible, searching always for the new, emphasizing the great value of originality . . . [and t]o create a market for the students' work" (Dunn 1937). However, the federal government's institutionalization of Indian art instruction lead to a dogma of traditional Indian painting, and The Studio style of painting was quite distinct, defined by flat areas of soft color contrasted with careful outlines (Archuleta 1991).

With the support of the department of Indian education, Dunn organized national and international exhibitions to promote The Studio and its students. As a result, the program soon received the patronage of numerous wealthy individuals. Several outstanding collections of Indian painting have at their core artwork produced by The Studio's students. Many of these students continued their artistic careers as artists upon graduation, including Allan Houser, Chiricahua Apache, and Pablita Velarde, Santa Clara Pueblo, who influenced generations of Indian painters. —ARCHULETA

"SHOW WHAT AN INDIAN CAN DO"

Sports

IN OCTOBER 1997, GRACE THORPE CAME TO the small central Pennsylvania town of Carlisle with a petition. Usually when she is engaged in political activism of this nature, Thorpe is rallying to protect the environment from nuclear waste. But this time was different. She had come to collect signatures to endorse her father, Jim Thorpe, as the century's premier athlete. Jim Thorpe, Sac and Fox, had been a major league baseball player, Olympic gold medalist in the decathlon and the modern pentathlon, professional football player, and founding member of the organization that became the National Football League. In fact, the Associated Press had, in 1950, named Jim Thorpe the greatest athlete of the first half of the twentieth century. The next fifty years, however, would usher in the era of televised sports, and after a half-century of visual exposure and sports marketing hype, sports fans had all but forgotten the great

Backfield at
Carlisle Indian
School, 1912.
Shown left to right
are Alexander
Arcasa, Stansil
Powell, Gus Welsh,
and Jim Thorpe.

PHOENIX INDIAN
5 - 128
PHYS. ED.

athletes who performed before the miracle of instant replay. Grace Thorpe felt that it was important to remember her father and his athletic achievements. "I just think he was the greatest all-around athlete of the century," she said, "and I just felt I can do something about that."

Jim Thorpe's daughter chose to stop in Carlisle on her petition drive because Carlisle was one of the most important places in her father's life. Thorpe first achieved national recognition playing football and running track for Carlisle Indian School. Some people might be puzzled that a committed political activist would put this kind of effort into a sports poll, but her work on behalf of Jim Thorpe's legacy testifies to the significance of sports history at boarding schools such as Carlisle, and among Native Americans generally. Mainstream sports, such as football, were first introduced at boarding schools as part of a larger effort to erase Native American culture and history from memory. Ironically, sports became a source of pride for students and their children, a resource for pleasure, and an instrument through which they creatively constituted and reformulated their identities.

Baseball team, Flandreau Indian School, South Dakota, ca. 1900.

When sports were first developed as part of boarding school curricular and extracurricular programs, they were meant to support the schools' goal of convincing white skeptics (many of whom believed in the biological inferiority of those they considered non-white) that Native Americans could become assimilated. Physical education programs for girls, for example, stressed exercises to "correct" body posture and racially transform the girls by erasing physical evidence of American Indian background. Ironically, boarding schools developed some of the most popularly recognized athletic programs of the first half of the twentieth century. Sports were much more than tools for assimilation or evidence of Indian success. Sports formed a complex popular culture that students, boarding school administrators, and the Bureau of Indian Affairs (BIA) struggled with one another to define.

Beginning in the mid-1890s, Carlisle football teams competed successfully against national powerhouse collegiate programs of the time. In 1899, the school hired legendary coach Glenn S. "Pop" Warner, who led Carlisle's football teams to tremendous success over the next fifteen years.

JIM THORPE

Legendary Sac and Fox athlete Jim Thorpe (1888?–1953), whose Native name was Wo-tho-huck or "Bright Path," was born near Prague, Indian Territory (now the state of Oklahoma). He entered Carlisle Indian School in 1907. He played football for Carlisle until 1909, when he left school to work in North Carolina, where he played semi-pro baseball for one season. He returned to Carlisle in 1911, leading the football team to successful seasons. He was named to the All-American football team in 1911 and 1912.

In 1912 Thorpe represented the U.S. in the Olympic games held in Stockholm, Sweden. He was the first athlete to win both the decathlon and pentathlon in the Olympics. When King Gustav V of Sweden presented Thorpe with his two gold medals, he declared, "You, Sir, are the greatest athlete in the world." One year later, the International Olympic Committee (IOC) stripped Thorpe of his medals, charging that the semi-pro baseball he had played invalidated his amateur status. Thorpe went on to play professional baseball and professional football, and became president of the American Professional Football Association in 1920. The Associated Press named him

"The Greatest Male Athlete of the First Half-Century" in 1950, three years before he passed away. Thorpe was inducted into the National Indian Hall of Fame; the Professional Football Hall of Fame in Canton, Ohio; the National Track and Field Hall of Fame; and the Pennsylvania and Oklahoma Halls of Fame.

Thorpe's family and friends petitioned the IOC for many years to reaffirm Thorpe's amateur status and reissue his 1912 gold medals. The IOC finally relented in 1982, recasting the medals and presenting them to Thorpe's family. In 1987, the family donated the medals to the Oklahoma Historical Society, and they were placed on display in the state capitol rotunda. No athlete has ever equaled Thorpe's success in three sports—football, baseball, and track and field—and no athlete has ever broken his record of winning both the decathlon and the pentathlon in the Olympic games. —LOMAWAIMA

The school also claimed some of the biggest sports stars of its era. Olympic silver medal distance runner Lewis Tewanima, Hopi, and Baseball Hall of Fame pitcher Charles Albert "Chief" Bende, Ojibwe, both played for Carlisle's teams. When Carlisle closed in 1918, Haskell assumed national prominence in football, particularly during the 1920s, when its teams traveled to play in Yankee Stadium. The Haskell football team generated enough publicity to finance the construction of a ten-thousand-seat football stadium on the Haskell campus. The success did not stop there. By 1950, long after Carlisle had closed, and after Haskell had ended its high-profile football program, federally operated boarding schools for Native Americans produced nationally recognized amateur boxers, along with highly successful high school teams in baseball, girls' and boys' basketball, volleyball, and track—teams that dominated competition within their regions.

Baseball team, U.S. Indian School, Fort Totten, North Dakota, 1913. According to a photo caption of the time, the Fort Totten team played "the fastest game in the state."

Richard Henry Pratt, who founded Carlisle in 1879, expressed distaste for football early on, at times portraying it as brutal, corrupt, and dishonest. He eventually embraced the game, realizing that sports provided a more potent public relations tool than he could have imagined when he first opened the school's doors. Football promoted a popular image of male Native Americans as controlled and civilized, able to compete in the modern world with masculine aggressiveness under the leadership of a white coach (like Warner, stern and paternal) while behaving with the temperate modesty of gentlemen.

Girls in gymnasium, Haskell Indian School, Lawrence, Kansas, early 1900s. As the minds of the students were being shaped, so were their bodies.

On the other hand, Carlos Montezuma, Yavapai, the famed Pan-Indian leader and Native American medical doctor, staunchly supported Pratt's positive opinion of football, only to change his mind in later years. In the 1890s Montezuma served as the Carlisle football squad's team M.D. After a victory over the University of Wisconsin in Chicago in December of 1896, Montezuma praised football, writing from that city to Pratt:

> I can give no words that will express the amount of good
> . . . Carlisle is doing for the rising generation of the Indians
> by your football team and band coming to Chicago. . . . The
> press club—the pulse of Chicago—has had their eyes opened
> and now they understand Carlisle as never before. . . . They
> thought at first the team was coming only for what money
> there was in it, but now they see different. It was only to
> make a way into their hearts, so that they may realize their
> obligation to the Indian children for education and freedom
> into their enlightenment. (Larner 1983)

Yet sports also created problems for those who advocated the assimilation of indigenous people through the boarding school program. Just as federal policymakers wavered in their ideas about Native American education, they, along with school administrators and superintendents, often changed course when dealing with boarding school sports between 1890 and 1950. In November 1907, responding to a letter from a former Carlisle administrator who had written of corruption within the football program, Montezuma wrote an article, published nationally, on football at Carlisle. He cited specific instances of corruption within the school's athletic program, and harshly condemned Carlisle athletics for lack of professionalism.

Such allegations helped provide ammunition to senators from western states and others in Congress who were opposed to funding the boarding school program. In 1914, the House and Senate funded a joint congressional investigation into corruption and mismanagement at Carlisle. Former football star Gus Welch (whom coach Warner fondly remembered in a *Collier's* article

HIDDEN BALL TRICK

Pop Warner's Carlisle football teams not only won; they won with a unique sense of humor and irony that undercut pretensions of white superiority. The most famous example of this was the "hidden ball trick" employed against Harvard October 31, 1903. Setting up for a kickoff return, the Carlisle squad grouped around the player who caught the ball, who then tucked the pigskin under the jersey of a teammate. While the nation's intellectual elite groped around the field in chaos looking for the player with the ball, Carlisle's player scampered into the end zone with the football safely hidden from view. —BLOOM

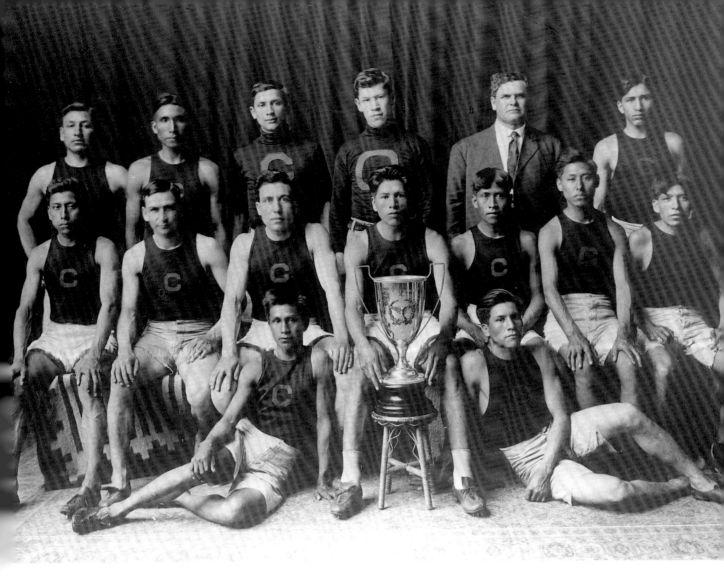

dated October 24, 1931, as "a highly intelligent Iroquois") led a petition drive signed by more than two hundred students that called for an investigation into the use of funds collected by the Carlisle Athletic Association, a body headed by Warner. They testified that Warner sold game tickets in hotels where the team stayed and, they suggested, kept the money; they told of the coach's common use of profanity; and they told detailed stories of Warner gambling on the team's performance.

Criticisms of boarding school sports programs intensified once again after 1928, when a commission headed by Lewis Meriam issued a scathing report criticizing the wretched conditions at many schools, the highly regimented forms of military discipline, and the lack of respect paid to diverse Native American cultures and traditions. Among the Meriam Report criticisms was a lack of time for free play and recreation (Meriam et al. 1928).

With the appointment of Will Carson Ryan, Jr., as director of education in the Indian Service in 1930, and John Collier as commissioner of Indian affairs in 1933, the BIA set out to

Carlisle track team, ca. 1910. Carlisle Indian School's winning track team featured Jim Thorpe (back row, center), Coach "Pop" Warner (back row, second from right, next to Thorpe), and Lewis Tewanima (second row, seated on the end at the right).

GYMNASIUM

Boys' basketball,
Haskell Indian
School, Lawrence,
Kansas, early 1900s.

reform the boarding school system, heeding many of the Meriam Report's recommendations. Ryan had, in fact, been a member of the Meriam team, and had authored the report's education chapter. The Collier administration was critical of the prominent position that sports held at boarding schools, noting in internal memos that the nationally acclaimed football teams at Haskell and Carlisle had always traveled in first-class comfort while other students had little recreation at all. Athletic teams brought fame and notoriety, and they generated tens of thousands of dollars in revenue for coaches and athletic association treasure chests, but they did little to help the average student. Collier and Ryan favored intramural athletics and recreation that would allow more free play and involve more students. These policy changes, along with other policies that lowered the average age of students, effectively ended the possibility that any Indian boarding school could field a high-profile football program.

Many Haskell alumni reacted bitterly to the decline in the status of the school's football team during the early 1930s. Sports that had once been a tool to promote assimilation had become a symbol of national pride for many Native Americans. In a series of articles he wrote for *Collier's* during the 1930s, Warner

Lewis Tewanima,
ca. 1908, with his
Olympic medal and
other trophies.

LEWIS TEWANIMA

Lewis Tewanima, Hopi, (whose name is also often spelled Louis, 1877–1969) achieved distinction as one of the greatest distance runners this country has ever produced. Tewanima attended Carlisle from 1907 to 1912 and was a member of the U.S. Olympic team in 1908, when he finished ninth in the marathon, and 1912, when he won a silver medal in the 10,000-meter run. In 1909 he established a world record in the indoor ten-mile run at Madison Square Garden. During this and most other races he exhibited the ability to change pace and sprint at regular intervals, a technique that discouraged other runners and usually left them far behind. Tewanima was selected as Helms Foundation member of the All-Time U.S. Track and Field Team in 1954. In 1972 he was inducted into the American Indian Athletic Hall of Fame (Oxendine 1988). —ARCHULETA

recalled that there was "a very real race pride" among the players he coached (Warner 1931) and Native American fans and supporters clearly felt similarly. High-profile boarding school football successfully pitted a racially defined group directly against white opponents in a way that has rarely been paralleled in United States sports history. By contrast, African-American athletes had fewer opportunities to compete against whites as a group. Black baseball players usually played in segregated leagues, only facing white teams in exhibitions or during the off-season in the Caribbean Island leagues. When they were finally allowed to play professional baseball with whites, they did so on integrated teams.

They were going to take me out of sports. . . . [They] tried to take away my letterman sweater, which I wouldn't let them do 'cause I paid for that. I said if I'm not going to be able to play sports then I'll leave.

Roy Dan Martinez, born 1929, Ottawa-Chippewa, attended Sherman (Heard Museum 1999)

Ironically, the decline of football in the 1930s left a void that schools soon filled with a new sport, one unquestionably more violent and brutal than football, and long associated with combat between ethnic groups: boxing. Boarding school boxing teams were extremely good; many Indian school boxers competed nationally in Amateur Athletic Union and Golden Gloves competitions. With boxing, school superintendents could continue to generate athletic revenues, and students found a new venue to experience pleasure and express pride.

In an interview for a 1995 oral history project, a successful former boxer from the Santa Fe Indian School discussed how boarding school had introduced him to people from different tribes, including Plains Indians, people from nearly every New Mexico Pueblo, Apaches, and Indians from the Pacific Northwest. When asked what motivated him to win in the ring and to overcome fear of getting hurt, he indicated an expansive understanding of Native American identity. "Well, I'll tell you, you got the pride. . . . If there's any race that's speaking different languages, outside of you, well you got the pride to demonstrate that you going to be in there fighting . . . with all that you have. Because you're an Indian, well, you going to show what an Indian can do" (Bloom 1995).

Letterman's sweater, Phoenix Indian High School, Arizona, 1968.

Lewis Bennet preparing for a game, Sherman Indian High School, Riverside, California, 1998.

Pride and pleasure mattered a great deal to students, especially those who attended boarding schools after 1933, when the new professed goals of respect toward Native American cultures did not always match students' actual experiences.

In interviews for the same oral history project, many former students remembered being allowed to speak only English while at school. An Ojibwe man who was sent to the Wahpeton boarding school in North Dakota in the early 1930s, and who later attended Pipestone Indian School in Minnesota, recalled being beaten for speaking his native language. He was first sent to Wahpeton at age five, when Ojibwe was his only language, but "they beat that out of you in a hurry, boy." A former Santa Fe Indian School boxer from the 1930s recalled that he was motivated in large part by a desire to beat up the boys' disciplinarian, a man named Stein. "I used to think about the time when I grew up. I said, 'I'm going to be a fighter. I'm going to tangle with that Mr. Stein'" (Bloom 1995).

Boxing spoke to the mischief and rebelliousness ever-present among boarding school students. In other interviews, former students remember the pleasure they derived at school from acts of chicanery. The man who was beaten for speaking Ojibwe told endless stories about pranks and petty theft that he and his friends conducted at Pipestone during the 1930s. Much as boarding school students joined dance clubs and school bands in order to participate in any form of entertainment sanctioned by school administrators, student boxers embraced their sport as an approved expression of rebellion. Students who were not boxers looked forward to boxing matches as social events that provided rare moments when they could behave in otherwise unsanctioned ways. Alumni recalled fights as exciting, fun-filled events that the student body looked forward to each week (Bloom 1995).

These social events were particularly important to students because sexuality was highly regulated at boarding schools. Even during the 1930s, when schools relaxed rules somewhat, girls and boys were often segregated at meal times or in classrooms, and dating was carefully monitored. Many of the pranks that alumni recalled in interviews involved breaking the rules that regulated sexuality. Boxing matches were social events that female and male students both attended. Spectators at these events felt free to express their emotions loudly and publicly. One of the Santa Fe boxers recalled in an interview that the atmosphere at Chilocco Indian School in Oklahoma was particularly wild, and so filled with tobacco smoke that his lungs hurt after the fight (Bloom 1995). A man who attended Chilocco

Seventh Annual Field Day trophy, Phoenix Indian School, Arizona, 1932.

Girls' basketball, Phoenix Indian School, Arizona, ca. 1902.

during the 1930s and later coached there remembers that people would drive over one hundred miles to attend fights at the school. Non-Indian spectators came from Oklahoma and Kansas. "There's something about it, about boxing. It's kind of like gambling, I guess, people were crazy about it! Boy, they just packed that gym" (Bloom 1995). BIA officials, however, worried about injury to and exploitation of students, and they feared boxing as a sport because it stirred up dangerous passions in the crowds.

For female students, participation in sports meant access to pleasure that was often denied to them in the course of their daily lives. Boarding schools attempted to maintain Victorian ideals well into the twentieth century, relegating female students to domestic courses of study and chores such as sewing, laundry, ironing, and cooking. Boarding schools monitored girls' activities much more closely than boys', and they also tended to allow boys a greater degree of participation in sports than they did girls. The high-profile athletic programs were created mostly for male students, though some schools did have girls' teams. Historian Sally Hyer (1990) has documented that female students at Santa Fe played a number of sports, including badminton, basketball, softball, and volleyball. Even so, many girls were frustrated by the limits on their participation in athletics. During a group interview with a gathering of Ojibwe men and women who attended the Pipestone Indian School in southwestern Minnesota during the 1930s, my questions about women's athletics turned into an opportunity to crack some jokes about the gender dynamics of boarding school life:

Girls' basketball
team, U.S. Indian
School, Fort
Totten, North
Dakota, ca. 1900.

Bloom: "Did girls have any sports when you were there? . . . "
Male former student: "Yeah. Trying to keep away from the boys."
[All laugh]
Female former student: "Track!"
Male: "That was your own track team." [More laughter]

Later in the interview, the female student recalled that there was not much emphasis on girls' physical education. "We would go in there and exercise. But I don't remember if there was any rigor daily, or even two or three times a week yet. I would say the boys had more opportunities for that than the girls did" (Bloom 1995).

Facing and below: Runners at the Lewis Tewanima Annual Race, 1999. For twenty years the challenging Tewanima Foot Race has been held during the Labor Day weekend in the village of Shungopovi at Second Mesa, Arizona. Runners come from all parts of the country to participate in ten-kilometer and five-kilometer races. The route begins at the north entrance of the village, goes down the mesa around the site of the old Hopi Day School, doubles back up the steep side of the mesa, and ends with a run through the houses of the village.

When students enjoyed boarding school sports, they did not always do so in ways that Anglo politicians and school administrators hoped for. The opportunity to win against whites at a fair fight helped some Native Americans to understand that bigger social losses came about as a result of battles that were not fair. In addition, sporting events and other extracurricular activities provided opportunities for some to have fun and enjoy moments of pleasure that were difficult to carve out in the highly regimented daily routine of boarding school life. In these cases, sports, music, art, and other activities were not simply diversions, but very real opportunities for students to evade rules, and to claim time for themselves.

In December 1999, the cable sports network ESPN broadcast their list of the top ten North American athletes of the century. A panel of expert sports reporters placed Jim Thorpe at number seven, just below the great hockey player Wayne Gretzky, and just above the legendary baseball center fielder Willie Mays. Grace Thorpe did not get her wish to have her father ranked as number one. However, she did help to ensure that he was not forgotten. Her efforts are testimony to the powerful legacy of sports from federally operated boarding schools for Native Americans, a legacy that continues today in the popularity of games such as basketball on reservations, and in the legends and memories of women and men who attended boarding schools. ⌐

A DOMESTIC SCIENCE DINNER JUNE 1 PHOENIX INDIAN SCHOOL MESSINGER VI

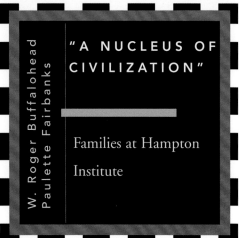

W. Roger Buffalohead
Paulette Fairbanks

"A NUCLEUS OF CIVILIZATION"

Families at Hampton Institute

MANY OF US THINK OF SCHOOLS AS PLACES for academic instruction, as places where we learn math, science, or English grammar. Federal Indian boarding schools were designed with much broader goals in mind—they were built to be places that would utterly transform Indian people. They were designed to obliterate tribal identity, to destroy Native languages, to eradicate Native religions. These goals dictated that school programs be designed to transform Indian homes, the heart of Indian communities.

Accordingly, domestic or home economics classes trained Indian girls in new standards and practices of menu planning, cooking, housekeeping, dress making, and child rearing—pushing aside Native foods, techniques to prepare and preserve foods, clothing styles and materials, architecture, and family structures. Materials developed for boarding school courses on "housewifery" painstakingly compared the pros and cons of wallpaper versus whitewash, wood-frame versus logs, and curtains versus shades. Trades training for boys introduced new standards and practices for making a living. New skills, especially those necessary for building and maintaining the new kinds of homes—carpentry, furniture building, plumbing, painting, and masonry—replaced ancient Native skills.

Native family structures were central targets of federal educational agendas. Schools intended to eliminate multiple wives and husbands, introduce Christian marriage practices, even change the ways parents expressed affection for, or disciplined, their children. One of the best examples of how Indian families and Indian homes were targeted for transformation was the model family program at Hampton Institute.

In contrast with other institutions in the federal Indian school system, Hampton was a private school for African Americans that began enrolling American Indians in 1878. Hampton's historic Indian education program, a "school within

Facing: Domestic science dinner, Phoenix Indian School, Arizona, June 1900. "Practice" dinners served many purposes. Girls received first-hand experience in meal preparation and service, while dinner "guests" practiced table manners.

Hampton Institute as seen across the Hampton River, 1878.

HAMPTON NORMAL AND AGRICULTURAL INSTITUTE

Samuel Chapman Armstrong, a son of New England missionaries to Hawai'i, established Hampton Institute in Hampton, Virginia, in 1868. Armstrong established the private, non-denominational school to train "the hand, the head and the heart" of select African-American youths "to be examples to, and teachers of, their people" (Ludlow 1888). Armstrong believed in a hierarchy of the races that firmly privileged whites over the black, yellow, red, and brown races. His goal at Hampton was to train black teachers, who would train black youth to remain in the South as menial laborers. The institute stressed work over academic training; Armstrong preferred the "blockhead at the blackboard" (Ludlow 1888) who labored hard in the field to the student who excelled academically, and who, in Armstrong's mind, aspired to an inappropriately high place in life.

In 1878, Richard Henry Pratt was searching for an eastern school that would accept twenty-two Indian students, the newly released prisoners of war he had been in charge of at Fort Marion, Saint Augustine, Florida. Arrested by the military during the Red River War on the Southern Plains, the hostages had spent three years in prison. Pratt had conducted an educational "experiment," enlisting teachers of English, Christian hymns, and "civilized" living to work with the POWS. Armstrong was happy to accept the enrollees at Hampton Institute in Hampton, Virginia. The "Indian department" continued until 1923, followed by the Indian Program that continues to recruit Indian students to the school today. —LOMAWAIMA

a school," provided English language and other instruction to students with limited exposure to "civilization" until 1923. One of the program's central components was a model family program, which focused on training young, married Indian couples.

The model family program was not large or long-lived; only twenty-three Indian families (fifteen Lakota, six Omaha, and two Winnebago or Oneida) took part between 1882 and 1891. We cannot even credit the model family program with really "transforming" the Indians who attended, for most of the Indian families who took part in the Hampton program had been influenced by other boarding schools or by missionaries and had already decided to adopt American lifestyles and values. The program seems to have helped them sustain their life choices, rather than changed their life choices. Despite these limitations, the model family program at Hampton offers a vivid image of what the federal government wanted Indian families to become, and it offers us vivid portraits of several Indian families doing their best to adapt and survive.

Anthropologist Alice Fletcher, a school supporter and policy reformer, spearheaded the model family program. Fletcher had "begged that Hampton receive a few married couples and train them in model housekeeping on such a scale as would be feasible on the reservations in the West" (Folsom 1918). In the summer of 1882, after traveling to Lakota/Dakota communities in Dakota Territory, and to the Omaha reservation, Fletcher headed east with the students she had recruited. When they arrived at Hampton on August 22 that year, they joined over eighty American Indian students on the campus, the majority Lakota/Dakota (Sioux).

Among the students who came to Hampton with Fletcher were the first two families of the model family program, Philip and Minnie Stabler and their young son Edward, and Noah and Lucy La Flesche. Fletcher had close ties to the La Flesches, an influential Omaha family, and Lucy La Flesche was the twenty-one-year-old daughter of Omaha chief Joseph La Flesche.

These families, and the small number who followed, were role models in the effort to "civilize" American Indians. Hampton school officials, like other reformers of the day, viewed the family as "the unit of Christian civilization" (Folsom 1918). As a campus publication noted of an Omaha couple trained at the school, "Here is a little unbroken family, a nucleus of civilization!" (*Southern Workman* April 1885).

My name is Lucy La Flesche, and I am here with my husband to go to school. . . . We came here last August. The first time I rode in [railroad] cars was when we were coming to Hampton. . . . I got very sick on the way. Everything I saw when we [were] coming seemed wonderful to me. . . . Twenty-seven of us came from the Omaha tribe, twenty-one stayed at Carlisle, and six of us came to Hampton.

LUCY LA FLESCHE (SOUTHERN WORKMAN AUGUST 1883)

Instructions in gender rituals, early 1900s. Victorian standards of manners and social graces were taught to students in the early days of the schools.

Stabler family at
Hampton, ca.
1882. Left to right:
Philip, Eddie, and
Minnie Stabler,
Omaha.

Trade school
carpentry, ca. 1890.
The husbands in
Hampton's model
family program were
trained primarily in
carpentry and
farming.

The married couples were initially housed in Winona Lodge, a dormitory built in 1882 to house American Indian female students. The husbands were trained in carpentry and were enrolled in the Indian department. Wives were instructed in "the various arts of home making and home keeping, and proved most earnest pupils" (Ludlow et al. 1893). Lucy La Flesche took classes in the Indian department, but later qualified for entry into the academic program. Minnie Stabler, twenty-two, received similar training, in addition to taking care of Edward. She wrote: "I work in [the] afternoon and go to school in the morning. I keep house myself and cook, wash, iron, sew, and scrub." (Hampton University Archives) *Southern Workman* noted of the wives, "The women can sew a little, but are not experts in taking care of rooms. They prefer to put the sheets on the outside of the bed, and blankets in the place of sheets. They are willing to learn however" (October 1882).

Southern Workman reported the arrival of the new students at Hampton, commenting: "Another important event is the arrival of . . . new students and one whose position in the School is not yet defined . . . a fine looking baby of eighteen months. In order that his future career may be watched, we give his name, Edward Stabler. He is said to be like all babies the world over, and speaks a language intelligible to the inhabitants of Babyland" (October 1882).

A few months after the two Omaha families arrived at Hampton, they were joined by Philip and Kate Counsellor, with their son Charles, from Dakota Territory's Lower Brule agency. Philip had attended a mission school, could read in Dakota, but did not speak English, while Kate, eighteen, had "not been much if any at school." Charles, described stereotypically as "a fine lit-

NOAH AND LUCY LA FLESCHE

Noah and Lucy La Flesche, Omaha, were among the first couples recruited to Hampton's model family program. Lucy had attended the Omaha Mission school from age ten to fourteen. When the first "Omaha Cottage" at Hampton was complete and the La Flesches moved in, they served guests lemonade and cake at an afternoon open house. Faculty member Josephine Richards described their home: "Let us trust its light will shine far off into many a crowded cabin and comfortless teepee, and transform them likewise into pure, sweet, Christian homes" (*Southern Workman* April 1884).

The La Flesches were back home in Nebraska by the summer of 1886. They built a home, the Union Cottage,

financed with a loan from the Women's National Indian Association. By 1895, however, they were renting the cottage and had moved into a cabin that Lucy owned. Contrary to the hopes of Hampton educators, Noah became interested in the Omaha dance house nearby, and Lucy was involved as well. By 1908, Noah was serving as headman of the Standing Hawk Lodge, a club dedicated to keeping up the Omaha songs and dances. In 1918, Lucy was "practically an invalid with rheumatism" and the following year after an Indian dance, Noah caught cold, developed pneumonia, and died (Hampton University Archives). —BUFFALOHEAD AND MOLIN

Baby Richard Tiaokasin, Standing Rock Lakota, with Edward Miller, Omaha, ca. 1918. The Hampton model family program included many young children, who either came to the school with their parents or were born during their parents' time there.

tle brave, who speaks English exactly as well as he does Dakota," was about one year old (*Southern Workman* February 1883). He and Edward Stabler accompanied their parents to some classes. The babies helped "to enliven the sewing-room, where they [were] left during their mothers' absence in the morning, and [were] kindly treated and waited upon by the girls, who [vied] with each other in caring for them" (Report of the Commissioner of Indian Affairs, 1883).

By 1883, school officials announced that benefactors had offered support to build two cottages on campus to house the Omaha couples. The dwellings, which the husbands helped to construct, were intended to be object lessons, to teach "how comfortable and attractive a house can be put up at small expense." School officials hoped the experiment would give

insight "into true home-keeping" (*Southern Workman* June 1884). A year later, when the cottages were nearly completed, they were described by faculty member Elaine Goodale: "They look like good-sized bay-houses almost, with the diminutive porch over the door, the inside finished with really artistic paneling of brown cartridge paper divided by raised lines of dark-red; the tent-like ceiling, the three tiny, pretty, well-cupboarded rooms" (*Southern Workman* March 1884).

The La Flesche, Stabler, and Counsellor families were the only participants in the model family program until 1884, when five other couples arrived at the school. Among them were three couples recruited by Hampton faculty member Cora Mae Folsom and the newly married Reverend and Mrs. John J. Gravatt, who had been sent to Dakota Territory to recruit new students. During that trip, the recruiters had visited Minniconjou leader Hump's community, where a "large tipiful of fine looking old men" met in council to consider the purpose of their visit (Folsom 1918). The Reverend Gravatt, who was the Hampton chaplain, sought with the help of an interpreter to persuade the tribal leaders "that the time had come to prepare their children to cope with the white man by using the white man's weapons." The councilmen, however, responded: "They have taken away our tobacco and we will give up our rations; we will *not* give up our children" (emphasis in original). Folsom described:

> They were very courteous but very firm. Crowds of men and women had collected around the tipi and when we came out feeling like chastened children we had to pass down a long line of blanketed Indians, some of whom responded to our smiling "How" while others looked pained and grieved to see women so young and so apparently innocent ready to tear little children from the loving arms of their parents. They had seen to it, however, that there was nothing to tear, for not a child of the five hundred appeared in sight to tempt us. Where so many could have hidden in tipis so devoid of hiding places we shall never know, but the children must have been in the game for no sound of them reached our ears. (Folsom 1918)

The Gravatts and Folsom visited other Dakota Territory communities, eventually recruiting students from Cheyenne River, Crow Creek, Lower Brule, and Yankton agencies. A short time after the group's arrival at Hampton, *Southern Workman* reported the establishment of an advanced class in the Indian

Facing: Fire Cloud family at Hampton, 1885. The majority of the participants in the model family program were Lakota/Dakota. The Fire Clouds, Crow Creek Lakota, brought two sons with them to Hampton, joining two sons already at the school, Front row, left to right: Daniel, Emma, Walter. Back row, left to right: Daniel Jr., Tommy, James.

department, attended by men and women "who are in earnest, and are fitting themselves for teachers or for the ministry" (January 1885).

In 1885, five more families arrived at the school, among them Daniel and Emma Fire Cloud, "a [Lakota] family of four whose magnet at Hampton has been the two little sons who have been doing well in the school for the last two years" (*Southern Workman* May 1885). "Their arrival," a report noted, "completed the family group. . . . The joy of these little ones on being told that their father and mother would soon be with them was most touching and the meeting between the long separated parents and children was a scene not easily forgotten" (*Southern Workman* June 1885). The Fire Clouds, who also had a child born to them at the school, became the largest family in the program. Reflecting the ill health pervasive during the period, two of their sons died at Hampton, including their newborn child, and Emma succumbed to tuberculosis shortly after the family's return home. Daniel, who had "for some time been sexton and lay reader in the Episcopal church" at Crow Creek, continued that work following his tenure at Hampton (*Southern Workman* July 1886).

In April 1885, *Southern Workman* reported that ground had been broken for two new cottages, which were to be occupied by Lakota families. The Omaha cottages, the publication noted, "formed a centre for those from that tribe, as the Sioux, now building, will for theirs" (*Southern Workman* June 1885). Eventually six cottages were built at Hampton for the model family program, forming an area on campus that became known as "The Reservation." These dwellings and the families who lived in them attracted the attention of tourists and other visitors. As reported in *Southern Workman:*

> Two of the cottages particularly are kept as neat as wax, and are truly object lessons to all who enter them, whether they are skeptical tourists who fancy it an impossibility for Indians to be tidy, or the other scholars who contrast these homes with very different log cabins and tipis to be found on a Western Reserve. (June 1887)

The outside area included a "modest lawn" in front, separated from a road by a low fence. The fence was intended to discourage, "however vainly," the "very enterprising" little children within from "perilous voyages of discovery to the Steam Laundry, the Gas House, and other points of Interest." The cottage occupants laid out "tiny gardens" to grow vegetables for their meals and the men also planted potatoes in the larger school garden (Hampton Normal and Agricultural Institute 1887–1888).

Folsom commented that "The care and training of single boys and girls has its problems but it's the witches' song of, 'Double, double, care and trouble' for married children" (1918). The cares for faculty members included settling marital disputes that sometimes broke out:

> Naturally, the course of true love did not always run smoothly. I once received a request from a perturbed husband: "Please talk to her." His wife had been unhappy and had concluded she would prefer Winona [Lodge] to her cottage home. It was a talk to him, however, which seems to have lingered in my memory as, armed with the Episcopal prayer book—they belonged to that church—I paid him a call. Happily the trouble soon blew over. (Folsom 1918)

According to school reports, one couple "had been married by force and were not at all congenial or happy together. After several months of domestic unhappiness here they were returned [home] to separate" (Ludlow et al. 1893). Another couple was deemed "mismatched" by Hampton personnel.

Most of the faculty in Hampton's Indian department were single, Euro-American females. Their unmarried state "never ceased to interest" the Indian students, who often asked the women why they had not married. The students also speculated about a teacher's marriage prospects, or offered sympathy with comments such as: "Never mind . . . perhaps you [will get a husband] by and by," "[You're a] pretty girl, I think somebody [will] have you after [a] while," or "Pray [to] God, He [will] get you one" (that is, a husband) (Folsom 1918).

Hampton officials promoted church- and state-sanctioned marriage customs, approving, for example, when alumni sent formal invitations announcing Christian ceremonies. Citizenship acquired through allotment policies required adherence to new laws, including marriages recognized as legal by American authorities. Folsom stated that the school eventually received "announcements of engagements, wedding cards and newspaper accounts of church weddings as minutely described as are those of the more advanced race" (1918). She also described her first experience attending such a wedding of a student who had returned home:

> The prospective bride and groom on this occasion were seated apart during the service preceding the ceremony, and when called upon to come forward, went straggling down the aisle, one far ahead of the other, and took their places before the white clergyman at the chancel, a stove pipe between them. After the ceremony was over they proceeded in similar

fashion to their respective seats in the congregation, and at the close of the service[,] the groom, never once glancing at his bride, conversed a few moments with me, then jumped on his horse and was soon lost of sight, while the bride, in her bright blue wedding shawl, seemed perfectly satisfied with the proceedings, and after lengthy congratulations—or their equivalent—proceeded with her parents to her new home. (Folsom 1918)

Folsom, who was "inexpressibly shocked" by the proceedings, found herself "quite alone in such a sentiment; to everyone else it seemed a great step in civilization."

The Stablers—"the faithful and hard-working husband, the neat and smiling housekeeper, the 'Eddy' who loved everybody and whom everybody loved"—completed their three-year term at Hampton and returned home to the Omaha agency in Nebraska in spring 1885. They had become "so much a part of the life" at Hampton, "their little home such a pleasant centre," that they would be sorely missed (*Southern Workman* April 1885). Nevertheless, hopes were high for their success:

> But how safe we feel about them! With what anxious hearts we have seen some go out—sick or inefficient ones, young girls and boys with unformed minds and half-disciplined natures to meet such a terribly uncertain future! Here is a little unbroken family, a nucleus of civilization! Philip Stabler goes to plant his own fields, to build his own house; and Minnie, and her boy we know, can make that house a home. (*Southern Workman* April 1885)

By the time the Stablers left Hampton for home, plans had been made to extend the "civilized" housing of married couples to the reservations. In a speech in September 1884, Alice Fletcher had spoken of the need for "civilized" homes for Indians. She criticized the educational system for instructing Indian students in new habits and then sending them home, where tribal traditions held fast. "We educate them for civilization," said Fletcher, "and expect three years to overcome centuries of a fixed order of things." She advocated that more young Indian couples be trained in the East so that "after their return they might make civilized homes to be the centres of civilization among the tribes." Fletcher also suggested that such families be provided with support "to start civilized homes" (Fletcher 1884).

Fletcher's scheme of building "civilized" reservation homes found support among members of the Women's National Indian Association (WNIA), an organization of white women. Moved

Facing: Stabler family at Omaha Agency, ca. 1893. Eddie, the oldest child, stands in the immediate foreground, with Philip behind him; Minnie and the two little girls, Cora and Sara, are seated in a wagon. The child at left in front is unidentified.

PHILIP, MINNIE, AND EDWARD STABLER

Philip and Minnie Stabler left their home at the Omaha Agency in Nebraska in 1882 to attend Hampton Institute. They arrived with their young son Eddie, and Philip's nephew, Gus Stabler. After three years at Hampton, they returned home, where they were the first Hampton family to receive an interest-free home-building loan from the Connecticut Indian Association. The association maintained tight control over all aspects of construction. To purchase building materials, Philip had to send them an itemized statement, authenticated and signed by a local missionary. The total cost of Connecticut Cottage, reduced by Philip's labor and the elimination of a brick cellar, was $367.49. The association insured the structure against windstorms, cyclones, and tornadoes.

Philip and Minnie made regular payments on their home, but in 1894 Philip died, and a few years later Minnie "had to rent the home [they] worked so hard to complete." Eddie, their oldest child, passed away in 1912. Minnie sold some of her land and "built a very good new house" (Hampton University Archives).

— BUFFALOHEAD AND MOLIN

to action by Fletcher's speech, Sara T. Kinney, president of the WNIA's Connecticut auxiliary, worked to build support for the plan. Armed with approval from Commissioner of Indian Affairs Hiram Price, Kinney persuaded members of the Connecticut Indian Association to support Fletcher's ideas: "These suggestions of Miss Fletcher's did not chance to fall by the wayside, nor among thorns, nor yet upon stony places; but they did fall between the stones, into rich soil, where they took root, and flourished, and brought forth fruit" (Kinney 1889).

To Kinney and other reformers, the idea of home conveyed "the picture of one roof sheltering father and mother, and their children, secure in the sharing and inheritance of the property resulting from the toil of the family." They believed that the tribal extended kinship organization, communal ownership of land,

and rights of inheritance had to be dismantled. Kinney emphasized that this kinship organization, which constituted the true "tribal relation," could "only be broken by giving to the members of the tribe individual ownership of land and homes, and extending over these lands and homes our laws of property and legal descent" (Kinney 1889). Wherever this was done through the allotment of lands in severalty, according to Kinney, "the grip of the 'tribal relation' has been loosened, and the way opened for the founding of the [nuclear] family and the upbuilding of the home" (Kinney 1889).

Influenced by Hampton's model family program and the home building effort undertaken by the Connecticut Indian Association, the Women's National Indian Association, in November 1885, unanimously approved the adoption of the national Indian home building and loan department, with Kinney in charge. Money was loaned to Noah La Flesche in the amount of five hundred dollars. In November 1886, the La Flesches completed their new home, which they called Union Cottage, on allotted land near the Stablers' Connecticut Cottage. Kinney reported that seventeen applications for loans were received between November 1886 and November 1887. Two homes were built and nine applicants were assisted in enlarging or completing homes under construction. The home building and loan department provided grants to build houses and smaller sums, from five to one hundred dollars, to purchase items such as farm implements

Facing: Connecticut Cottage, Omaha Agency, Nebraska, n.d. The Stabler family's cottage was constructed in 1885–1886 with support from the Connecticut Indian Association.

Below: Omaha earth lodge, n.d. This lodge was identified as Philip Stabler's former home at the Omaha Agency in Nebraska.

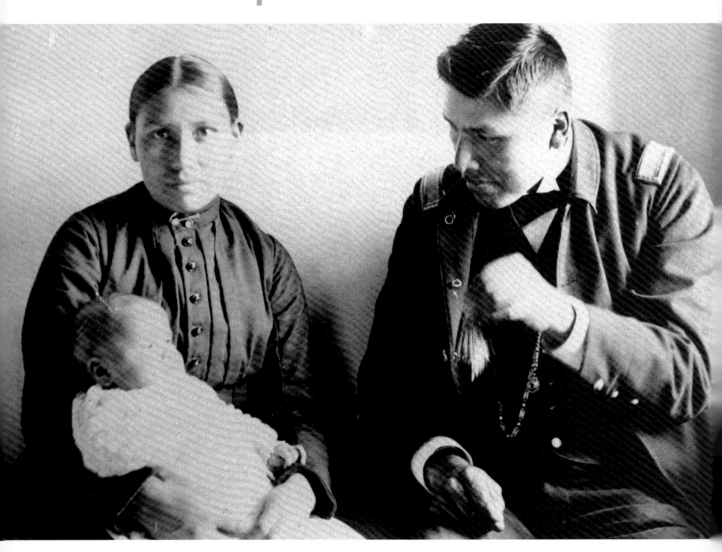

Bear family at
Hampton, 1889.
Cora Bear holds baby
Thomas Morgan as
John Bear looks on.
The Nebraska
Winnebago couple's
son was born at
Hampton when
Commissioner of
Indian Affairs
Thomas J. Morgan
was visiting the
school.

and cooking utensils (Kinney 1889). The loan recipients were very carefully selected, and Kinney and her committee members sought the advice and approval of missionaries, teachers, and agents before providing assistance.

Hampton's experiment in educating families at the school lasted for less than a decade, its demise attributed, in part, to the "outlay of extra care and expense" and to the increase of "civilized" homes in reservation communities. The WNIA's home building and loan department was also short-lived, eliminated in the early years of the twentieth century for related factors. At Hampton, the kindergarten classes started in 1886 for young Indian children were no longer needed, while other uses were found for the "Reservation" cottages—one became a housekeeping cottage for Indian girls.

Hampton's model family program for American Indians is probably best understood as a novel social and educational experiment with little impact on most Indian communities. The program was novel because it focused on the assimilation of a family unit, rather than the individual. Its impact was limited because of the small number of families who took part and the short amount of time the program lasted.

At the time the model family program operated, there was little understanding of Indian families or the role of the family in tribal cultures or communities. Indeed, most people working in Indian Affairs in the late nineteenth century held Indian family and community life in contempt, and viewed Indian social customs as the enemy of the educational efforts to assimilate Indians into American life. What Indian agents, educators, and missionaries called "returning to the blanket," however, Indian people saw as a return to normal family and community life. In fact, Indian family and community life has played a key role in the preservation of tribal languages and culture over time.

When the Hampton "model families" returned home, they often selectively integrated Native and "modern American" lifestyles. They joined other Indian families who also had chosen to cooperate, to some degree, with BIA directives and who had chosen to adopt, to some degree, the new habits and practices introduced in boarding schools. The Bureau of Indian Affairs typically referred to these families as "Progressives," and held them up as shining examples of the progress of "civilized living," despite resistance from so-called "Traditionals." This simple-minded dichotomy did not really capture the complexities of Native communities, but government officials have often been oblivious to the realities of Indian life. Indian people continued to negotiate real life, to adapt and to survive, and to build their own definitions of "model families." Indian homes today are a diverse, rich intermingling of traditions and innovations. The legacies of schools such as Hampton live on, but often in forms that Richard Henry Pratt, Samuel Chapman Armstrong, or Alice Fletcher might never have imagined. ⮑

AFTERWORD

Sherman Indian High
School cheerleaders,
Sherman Indian School
Reunion and Open
House, Riverside,
California, 1999.

THE HEARD MUSEUM EXHIBIT THAT INSPIRED
this publication remembers a chapter in American Indian history in ways that traverse borders of time and tribe, even when whole paragraphs and profound passages are sometimes forgotten in the telling. Still, we remain committed to exploring and interpreting a wide range of human experiences that touched the lives, often with pain, of the generations since 1879. The faces of the Sherman Indian School cheerleaders demand that we bring Indians into focus through a panoramic lens, and picture them as thoroughly modern people. Beyond doubt, the relatively small number of boarding schools in existence today are radically different places than Carlisle of yesteryear.

Reformers and policymakers considered Indian boarding schools obsolete institutions long before 1930. The Great Depression, the problem of distance for rural populations, and the molasses pace of public school integration yoked Indians to boarding schools for many years to come. Some young people chose boarding schools when discrimination in public schools became unbearable. In time, a few tribes claimed boarding schools as their own. The Santa Fe Indian School, founded in 1890 at the apex of assimilation, is operated today by the All Indian Pueblo Council in New Mexico. Chilocco and Phoenix persevered long enough to educate the grandchildren of original students before closing in the 1980s and 1990s. Flandreau in South Dakota lives on as one of the oldest operating Indian boarding schools in the United States.

Assimilation through education, which unsuccessfully tried to erase the influence of American Indian families and destroy communities, may be viewed in a global context. Canada's policy of forced assimilation through education mirrored that of the United States and lasted even longer. In Canada, a national dialogue on residential schools proceeded from a series of troubling court cases in British Columbia that exposed physical and sexual abuse of Native children. In Australia, the "stolen generation,"

Aboriginal children removed from their homes and families to be adopted by non-Indians, were victims of the same impulse that dominated U.S. policy at the turn of the century. Aboriginal people in Australia demanded the national government apologize to them for forcibly destroying families with the "Sorry Day" movement of recent years. So far the Australian government has not acknowledged remorse, though states and citizens have apologized and thousands signed "Sorry Books."

In the United States, no such dialogue has emerged. It is our hope that the museum exhibit and book will promote conversations about Native peoples' boarding school experiences. Native voices must be heard in the conversation—in thay way, we will enrich our view of America's past, present, and future.

Brenda Child

REFERENCES

Archuleta, Margaret and Rennard Strickland. 1991. *Shared Visions: Native American Painters and Sculptors in the Twentieth Century.* Phoenix: Heard Museum.

Berthrong, Donald. 1994. Jesse Rowlodge: Southern Arapaho as Political Intermediary. In *Between Indian and White Worlds: The Cultural Broker,* edited by Margaret C. Szasz. Norman: University of Oklahoma Press.

Blackhoop, Frank David. 1935. Letter to Hampton Staff, December 9. Hampton University Archives.

Blair, C.M. 1923. Records of the Superintendent of Chilocco School, National Archives, Record Group 75.

Bloom, John. 1995. Unpublished interviews conducted in Minnesota, New Mexico, and Oklahoma over five months (January–May) with graduates of Chilocco, Flandreau, Fort Wingate, Intermountain, Pipestone, and Santa Fe Indian Schools.

Burke, Charles H. 1923. "To All Indians," February 24. National Archives, Record Group 75.

Carlisle Indian School booklet. 1908. Cumberland County Historical Society, Carlisle, Pennsylvania.

Child, Brenda J. 1996. Runaway Boys, Resistant Girls: Rebellion at Flandreau and Haskell, 1900–1940. *Journal of American Indian Education* 35(3): 49–57.

———. 1998. *Boarding School Seasons: American Indian Families, 1900–1940.* Lincoln: University of Nebraska Press.

Chilocco Indian School Journal #6. 1938. Chilocco, Oklahoma.

Chilocco, Oklahoma: School of Opportunity for Indian Youth (pamphlet). Chilocco Printing Department. National Archives, Record Group 75.

Chilocco Indian Agricultural School. 1934. Annual Report. National Archives, Record Group 75.

Coleman, Michael C. 1994. American Indian School Pupils as Cultural Brokers: Cherokee Girls at Brainerd Mission, 1828–1829. In *Between Indian and White Worlds: The Cultural Broker,* edited by Margaret C. Szasz. Norman: University of Oklahoma Press.

Curtis, Natalie. 1920. An American Indian Artist. *The Outlook,* 14 January.

De Cora, Angel. 1908. The Department of Indian Art (booklet). Carlisle, Pennsylvania: Carlisle Indian School.

———. 1910. An Autobiography. *The Red Man,* March: 279–285.

——— (Mrs. Angel de Cora Dietz). 1911. Native Indian Art. Paper presented at First Annual Conference of the American Indian Association, 12–15 October, Ohio State University, Columbus.

Deloria, Philip. 1998. *Playing Indian.* New Haven, Connecticut: Yale University Press.

Dobkins, Rebecca. 1997. *Memory and Imagination: The Legacy of Maidu Indian Artist Frank Day.* Oakland: Oakland Museum of California.

Dunn, Dorothy. 1937. The Classes in Painting and Design (notes). Dorothy Dunn Archives, Laboratory of Anthropology, Museum of New Mexico 93DDK.171.

Eastman, Elaine Goodale. 1919. In Memoriam: Angel de Cora. *American Indian Magazine,* Spring.

Ellis, Clyde. 1999. " 'We Don't Want Your Rations, We Want This Dance': The Changing Use of Song and Dance on the Southern Plains." *Western Historical Quarterly* (30): 133–154.

Embree, Edwin R. 1939. *Indians of the Americas.* New York: Houghton Mifflin and Riverside Press.

Fisher, Dexter. 1979. Zitkala Sá: The Evolution of a Writer. *American Indian Quarterly* 5(3): 229–238.

Fletcher, Alice. 1884. Second Annual Address to the Lake Mohonk Conference of the Friends of the Indian, September, Lake Mohonk, New York. Philadelphia: Executive Committee of the Indian Rights Association.

Folsom, Cora. 1918. Indian Days at Hampton (unpublished manuscript). Hampton University Museum and Archives.

Green, Rayna. 1975. The Pocahontas Perplex: The Image of Indian Women in American Culture. *The Massachusetts Review* 16(4): 698–714.

————. 1988. The Tribe Called Wannabee: Playing Indian in Europe and America. *Folklore* (England), 99: 30–35. Reprinted 1995 in *Contemporary Cherokee Prose Writing,* edited by Joseph Bruchac, Greenfield Center, New York: Greenfield Review Press.

————. 1989. "Kill the Indian and Save the Man": Indian Education in the United States. In *To Lead and To Serve: American Indian Education at Hampton Institute, 1878–1923,* edited by Mary Lou Hultgren and Paulette Fairbanks Molin. Charlottesville: Virginia Foundation for the Humanities and Public Policy.

————. 1994. The Image of the Indian in American Popular Culture. In *The Handbook of North American Indians IV,* edited by Wilcomb Washburn. Washington, D.C.: Smithsonian Institution Press.

Hampton Normal and Agricultural Institute. 1887–1888. Annual Report. Hampton University Archives, Hampton, Virginia.

Hampton University Archives. Hampton University, Hampton, Virginia.

Heard Museum. 1999. Unpublished interviews conducted by Tessie Naranjo and Margaret Archuleta over three years (beginning in 1996) with various Indian boarding school alumni.

Hopi: Songs of the Fourth World. 1984. Produced by Pat Ferrero. Film. San Francisco, California: Ferrero Films.

Hyer, Sally. 1990. *One House, One Voice, One Heart: Native American Education at Santa Fe Indian School.* Santa Fe: Museum of New Mexico Press.

James, Harry C. 1974. *Pages from Hopi History.* Tucson: University of Arizona Press.

Johnston, Basil. 1989. *Indian School Days.* Norman: University of Oklahoma Press.

Kabotie, Fred. 1977. *Hopi Indian Artist.* Flagstaff: Museum of Northern Arizona and Northland Press.

Kelly, Lawrence C. 1983. *The Assault in Assimilation: John Collier and the Origins of American Indian Policy Reform.* Albuquerque: University of New Mexico Press.

Kinney, Sara T. 1889. *Helping Indians to Help Themselves.* Philadelphia: Dickson Printing Co.

Larner, J.W. 1983. *The Papers of Carlos Montezuma.* Wilmington, Delaware: Scholarly Resources.

Levchuck, Bernice. 1997. Within the Enemy: Challenge. In *Reinventing the Enemy's Language: Contemporary Native Women's Writings of North America,* edited by Joy Harjo and Gloria Bird. New York: W.W. Norton.

Lomawaima, K. Tsianina. 1994. *They Called It Prairie Light: The Story of Chilocco Indian School.* Lincoln: University of Nebraska Press.

————. 1996. Estelle Reel, Superintendent of Indian Schools, 1989–1910: Politics, Curriculum, and Land. *Journal of American Indian Education* 35(3): 5–31.

————. n.d. Indian Education: *By* Indians versus *For* Indians. In *Blackwell Companion to American Indian History,* edited by Philip Deloria and Neal Salisbury. Oxford: Blackwell Press. Forthcoming.

Ludlow, Helen, ed. 1888. *Ten Years' Work for Indians at the Hampton Normal and Agricultural Institute, Virginia.* Hampton, Virginia: Normal School Press.

Ludlow, Helen, et al. 1893. *Twenty-two Years' Work of the Hampton Normal and Agricultural Institute at Hampton, Virginia.* Hampton, Virginia: Normal School Press.

McAnulty, Sarah. 1976. Angel de Cora: American Indian Artist and Educator. *Nebraska History,* 57(2): 178–186.

Meriam, Lewis, et al. 1928. *The Problem of Indian Administration.* Institute for Government Research (Brookings Institute). Baltimore: Johns Hopkins Press.

Nüma-Nu (The Comanche People): A Photographic Exhibit of the Fort Sill Indian School Experience. 1981. Norman, Oklahoma: Cultures and Arts of Native Americans.

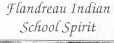

Flandreau Indian School Spirit

1994

SPIRIT

FLANDREAU INDIAN SCHOOL

1984

Nuu-chah-nulth Tribal Council. 1996. *Indian Residential Schools: The Nuu-chah-nulth Experience.* Port Albert, British Columbia: Nuu-chah-nulth Tribal Council.

Oxendine, Joseph B. 1988. *American Indian Sports Heritage.* Champaign, Illinois: Human Kinetics Books.

Prucha, Francis Paul, ed. 1990. *Documents of United States Indian Policy.* Second expanded edition. Lincoln: University of Nebraska Press.

Qöyawayma, Polingaysi (Elizabeth White). 1964. *No Turning Back.* Albuquerque: University of New Mexico Press.

Reel, Estelle. 1901. *Uniform Course of Study for the Indian Schools of the United States.* Washington, D.C.: Government Printing Office.

———. 1907. Annual Report of the Superintendent of Indian Schools. Washington, D.C.: Government Printing Office.

Report of the Commissioner of Indian Affairs. 1883. National Archives, Record Group 75.

Riney, Scott. 1999. *The Rapid City Indian School.* Norman: University of Oklahoma Press.

Rogers, John. 1974. *Red World and White: Memories of a Chippewa Boyhood.* Norman: University of Oklahoma Press.

Shaw, Dallas. 1922. Letters to Commissioner of Indian Affairs Charles Burke. National Archives, Record Group 75.

Society of American Indians. 1916. Constitution and By-Laws (handbook).

Society of American Indians: A National Organization of Americans (booklet). 1913.

Southern Workman. 1878–1939. Hampton, Virginia: Normal School Press.

Standing Bear, Luther. 1975 (1928). *My People the Sioux.* Lincoln: University of Nebraska Press.

Szasz, Margaret C. 1994. Samson Occom: Mohegan as Spiritual Intermediary. In *Between Indian and White Worlds: The Cultural Broker,* edited by argaret C. Szasz. Norman: University of Oklahoma Press.

Troutman, John W. 1999a. (In)Decent Amusements: The Practice and Politics of Music in Indian Country, 1900–1923 (unpublished paper). University of Texas at Austin.

———. 1999b. "Indian Blues" or "The Land of My Prairie Dreams"?: Tsianina Redfeather, Kiutus Tecumseh, and the Participation of Indians in American Popular Music, 1900–1930 (unpublished paper). University of Texas at Austin.

Utley, Robert M., ed. 1964. *Battlefield and Classroom: Four Decades with the American Indian, the Memoirs of Richard Henry Pratt.* New Haven, Connecticut: Yale University Press.

Warner, Glenn S. 1931. Heap Big Run-Most-Fast. *Collier's Weekly,* October 24: 18–19, 46. (Other installments of Warner's series of articles appeared in October 17 and October 31 issues of *Collier's Weekly.*)

RECOMMENDED FOR YOUNGER READERS

Eastman, Charles. 1972 (1917). *From the Deep Woods to Civilization.* Rapid City: Fenwyn Press Books.

Green, Rayna. 1992. *Women in American Indian Society.* New York: Chelsea House Publishers.

La Flesche, Francis. 1978 (1900). *The Middle Five: Indian Schoolboys of the Omaha Tribe.* Lincoln: University of Nebraska Press.

Milton, John R. 1972. *Oscar Howe.* Minneapolis: Dillon Press, Inc.

Reising, Robert. 1974. *Jim Thorpe.* Minneapolis: Dillon Press, Inc.

Santiago, Chiori. 1998. *Home to Medicine Mountain.* Berkeley: Children's Book Press.

Skolnick, Sharon and Manny Skolnick. 1997. *Where Courage is Like a Wild Horse: The World of an Indian Orphanage.* Lincoln: University of Nebraska Press.

Sterling, Shirley. 1998. *My Name is Seepeetza.* Toronto: Groundwood Books.

1995

U.S. Indian School (Fort Totten North Dakota), 61, 71
    sports at, 102, 112-113

Velarde, Pablita, 19, 97
violence, at boarding schools, 41-42
Virginia
    Hampton Indian School, 64, 65
    Hampton Institute, 58, 59, 117-129
    Hampton Normal and Agricultural Institute, 16, 117, 126

St. John's Episcopal Church Indian Choir, 83
vocational education, 17-18, 30-37, 78, 116

Waconda, Patricia, 26
Wade, J. C., 57
Wahpeton Boarding School (North Dakota), 110
Warner, Glenn S. "Pop," 101, 105, 106, 108
Wayquahgeshig, 24
Welch, Gus, 98, 99, 104-105

Wheelock, Dennison, 60
White, Elizabeth, 14, 16
Wild West Shows, 81
Wind on the Forehead, 64
women, stereotypes of, 30, 31, 82
Women's National Indian Association (WNIA), home building project, 128, 130-131, 132

Zurega, Ben, 42

PHOTOGRAPH SOURCES AND CREDITS

Page 1: National Archives and Records Administration, Northwest Regional Office, Seattle, L76-32-111. Page 2: Harvey W. Scott Memorial Library, Pacific University Archives, 12374. Page 4:(Background image) William Larrabee, photographer, Hampton University Archives, Hampton, Virginia. Page 7: Hampton University Archives, Hampton, Virginia. Page 12-13: South Dakota State Historical Society State Archives. Page 14-15 top: Library of Congress Collection. Page 15 bottom: Arizona Historical Foundation, University Libraries, Arizona State University, Tempe, Arizona, N-1110. Page 16: Owen Seumptewa, photographer, Heard Museum Library and Archives, Phoenix, Arizona. Page 17: William Larrabee, photographer, Hampton University Archives, Hampton, Virginia. Page 18: National Archives and Records Administration, Washington, D.C., 75-EXP-2B. Page 19: Sherman Indian High School Museum, Riverside, California. Page 20: National Archives and Records Administration, Northwest Regional Office, Seattle, L76-32-111. Page 21: National Archives and Records Administration, Washington, D.C., 75-PA-1-2. Page 23: Craig Smith, photographer, Heard Museum Library and Archives, Phoenix, Arizona. Page: 24: Harvey W. Scott Memorial Library, Pacific University Archives. Page 25 top: Harvey W. Scott Memorial Library, Pacific University Archives, 1583. Bottom: K. Tsianina Lomawaima Collection. Page 26: Craig Smith, photographer, Sherman Indian High School Museum, Riverside, California. Page 27 top: Arizona Historical Foundation, University Libraries, Arizona State University, Tempe, Arizona, N-1105. Bottom: Craig Smith, photographer, Heard Museum Library and Archives, Phoenix, Arizona. Page 28: Eastern Washington Historical Society, Cheney Cowles Museum, MS120 4.12.2#776. Page 30: Davidson, photographer, Harvey W. Scott Memorial Library, Pacific University Archives, No.42. Page 31: Eastern Washington Historical Society, Cheney Cowles Museum, MS 120#55. Page 32 top: National Archives and Records Administration, Washington D.C., 75-EXE-CROW-8D. Bottom: South Dakota State Archives, Pierre, South Dakota. Page 33 top: Hampton University Museum, Hampton, Virginia. Bottom: South Dakota State Archives, Pierre, South Dakota. Page 34 top left: Haskell Library and Archives, Haskell Indian Nations University, Bureau of Indian Affairs, Lawrence, Kansas. Bottom right: Craig Smith, photographer, Hampton University Museum, Hampton, Virginia. Page 35: Craig Smith, photographer, Private Collection. Page 36: Nancy B. McMahon Collection. Page 37 top right: Sherman Indian High School Museum, Riverside, California. Bottom left: Sherman Indian High School Museum, Riverside, California. Page 38: Drex Brooks, photographer, Sweet Medicine, University of New Mexico Press, Albuquerque, 1995. Page 39 top: Arizona Historical Foundation, University Libraries, Arizona State University, Tempe, Arizona, N-2809. Bottom: State Historical Society of Iowa, Iowa City. Page 40: Sherman Indian High School Museum, Riverside, California. Page 41: Cumberland County Historical Society, Carlisle, Pennsylvania, JO-1-4. Page 42: Heard Museum Library and Archives, Phoenix, Arizona. Page 43: Skip C. Lowery Collection. Page 44 left: Greg Lonewolf, photographer, Heard Museum Library and Archives,

Phoenix, Arizona. Right: Delbridge Honanie Collection. Page 45: Delbridge Honanie Collection. Page 46: Taber photo, Southwest Museum Collection, Los Angeles, California, N.20086. Page 47: K. Tsianina Lomawaima Collection. Page 50: Eastern Washington Historical Society, Cheney Cowles Museum, MS 120 5.1.14#822. Page 51 top: Brenda J. Child Collection. Page 53: Cumberland County Historical Society, Carlisle, Pennsylvania, PA-CH2-40. Page 54-55: Cumberland County Historical Society, Carlisle, Pennsylvania, 14-20A-2. Page 56: Kansas State Historical Society, Topeka, Kansas, FK2.D4 L.76 HI*65. Page 57: Kansas State Historical Society, Topeka, Kansas, FK2.D4 L.76 HI*66. Page 58: Craig Smith, photographer, Private Collection. Page 59: Craig Smith, photographer, Private Collection. Page 60: Cumberland County Historical Society, Carlisle, Pennsylvania, PA-CH1-v. Page 61 top: Craig Smith, photographer, Heard Museum Collection, Phoenix, Arizona, HM3515-2. Bottom: State Historical Society of North Dakota, 970.637 T641 1913. Page 62: Hampton University Archives, Hampton, Virginia. Page 63: Sherman Indian High School Museum, Riverside, California. Page 64-65: Hampton University Archives, Hampton, Virginia. Page 66 top: Craig Smith, photographer, Private Collection. Bottom: Arizona Historical Foundation, University Libraries, Arizona State University, Tempe, Arizona, N-1106. Page 67: Miller, photographer, Archives and Manuscripts Division of the Oklahoma Historical Society, Oklahoma City, Oklahoma, 10272. Page 68 top: John N. Choate, photographer, Cumberland County Historical Society, Carlisle, Pennsylvania, PA-CH-3-1. Bottom: Kansas State Historical Society, Topeka, Kansas, FK2.D4 L.76 HI*56. Page 69 top: John N. Choate, photographer, Cumberland County Historical Society, Carlisle, Pennsylvania, PA-CH-3-1. Bottom: DeVincent Collection, Archives Center, National Museum of American History, Smithsonian Institution. Page 70 top left: DeVincent Collection, Archives Center, National Museum of American History, Smithsonian Institution. Right: DeVincent Collection, Archives Center, National Museum of American History, Smithsonian Institution. Page 71: Kansas State Historical Society, Topeka, Kansas, FK2.D4 L.76 HI*67. Page 72: State Historical Society of North Dakota, 970.637 T641 1913. Page 73: Haskell Library and Archives, Haskell Indian Nations University, Bureau of Indian Affairs, Lawrence, Kansas. Page 74: Haskell Library and Archives, Haskell Indian Nations University, Bureau of Indian Affairs, Lawrence, Kansas. Page 75: Haskell Library and Archives, Haskell Indian Nations University, Bureau of Indian Affairs, Lawrence, Kansas. Page 76: Haskell Library and Archives, Haskell Indian Nations University, Bureau of Indian Affairs, Lawrence, Kansas. Page 77: Haskell Library and Archives, Haskell Indian Nations University, Bureau of Indian Affairs, Lawrence, Kansas. Page 78: Museum of New Mexico, Santa Fe, New Mexico, Neg. no. 11234. Page 80: Haskell Library and Archives, Haskell Indian Nations University, Bureau of Indian Affairs, Lawrence, Kansas. Page 81: Craig Smith, photographer, Heard Museum Library and Archives, Phoenix, Arizona. Page 82: Harold Hanson, photographer, One House, One Voice, One Heart, Hyer, Sally, Museum of New Mexico,

Santa Fe, 1990, p.62. Page 83: Hampton University Archives, Hampton, Virginia. Page 84: Cumberland County Historical Society, Carlisle, Pennsylvania. Page 85: Cumberland County Historical Society, Carlisle, Pennsylvania. Page 86: Hampton University Archives, Hampton, Virginia. Page 88 top and bottom: Hampton University Museum, Hampton, Virginia. Page 90: Albert A. Line, photographer, Cumberland County Historical Society, Carlisle, Pennsylvania. Page 91: Sherman Indian High School Museum, Riverside, California. Page 92: Craig Smith, photographer, Carol A. Hyeoma and Susie D. Hyeoma Collection. Page 93: Craig Smith, photographer, Heard Museum Library and Archives, Phoenix, Arizona. Page 94: The Newberry Library, Chicago, Illinois. Page 95: Heard Museum Library and Archives, Phoenix, Arizona. Page 96: Archives Collection, Museum of Indian Arts and Culture/Laboratory of Anthropology, Santa Fe, New Mexico, 93 DDK.059. Page 98-99: Cumberland County Historical Society, Carlisle, Pennsylvania. Page 99 bottom: Craig Smith, photographer, Private Collection. Page 100: South Dakota State Archives, Pierre, South Dakota. Page 102 bottom: State Historical Society of North Dakota, 970.637 T641. Top right: National Archives and Records Administration, Washington, D.C., 75-EXH-1C. Page 103: National Archives and Records Administration, Washington, D.C., 75-EXH-1C. Page 105: Cumberland County Historical Society, Carlisle, Pennsylvania. Page 106: National Archives and Records Administration, Washington, D.C., 75-EXH-1E. Page 107: Cumberland County Historical Society, Carlisle, Pennsylvania, 15-15-1. Page 109 top: Delbridge Honanie Collection. Bottom: Dorothy Grandbois, photographer, National Museum of the American Indian, Washington, D.C., P26527. Page 110: Craig Smith, photographer, Heard Museum Archives, Phoenix, Arizona. Page 111: Arizona Historical Foundation, University Libraries, Arizona State University, Tempe, Arizona, N-1108. Page 112-113: State Historical Society of North Dakota, 970.637 T641. Page 114: Owen Seumptewa, photographer, Heard Museum Library and Archives, Phoenix, Arizona. Page 115: Owen Seumptewa, photographer, Heard Museum Library and Archives, Phoenix, Arizona. Page 116: National Archives and Records Administration, Washington, D.C., 75-EXP-2F. Page 117: Hampton University Archives, Hampton, Virginia. Page 119: Watkins Community Museum, Lawrence, Kansas. Page 120: Hampton University Archives, Hampton, Virginia. Page 121: Hampton University Archives, Hampton, Virginia. Page 123: Hampton University Archives, Hampton, Virginia. Page 124: Hampton University Archives, Hampton, Virginia. Page 129: Hampton University Archives, Hampton, Virginia. Page 130: Hampton University Archives, Hampton, Virginia. Page 131: Hampton University Archives, Hampton, Virginia. Page 132: Hampton University Archives, Hampton, Virginia. Page 134: Owen Seumptewa, photographer, Heard Museum Library and Archives, Phoenix, Arizona. Page 136: Craig Smith, photographer, Heard Museum Library and Archives, Phoenix, Arizona. Page 137: Craig Smith, photographer, Heard Museum Library and Archives, Phoenix, Arizona.